the perfect

PERSIMMON

the perfect
PERSIMMON

HISTORY, RECIPES, AND MORE

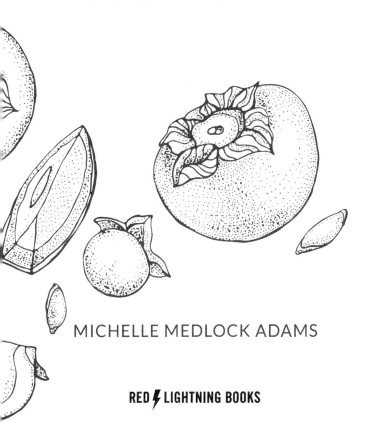

MICHELLE MEDLOCK ADAMS

RED ⚡ LIGHTNING BOOKS

This book is a publication of

RED LIGHTNING BOOKS

1320 East 10th Street
Bloomington, Indiana 47405 USA

redlightningbooks.com

Published in association with Cyle Young of
the Hartline Literary Agency, LLC.

Manufactured in the United States of America

ISBN: 978-1-68435-111-4
ISBN: 978-1-68435-112-1

1 2 3 4 5 25 24 23 22 21 20

This book is dedicated to my late mother-in-law, Martha Davis, who not only raised a wonderful son but also made the best persimmon pudding I've ever tasted. This one's for you, Martha.

CONTENTS

ACKNOWLEDGMENTS

*A*t may take a village to raise a child, but it takes an entire country to birth a book—especially this one. Because here's a little disclaimer for you: I'm not a great cook. (Those of you who know me well are nodding your heads in agreement.) Now, I'm an awesome baker. When it comes to sweet concoctions, I'm your gal. But some of the healthier main dishes, soups and salads, and side dishes featured in this book were a bit challenging for me. Thus, I had to rely on the people in my world who are my go-to kitchenistas when I had questions about ingredients, substitutions, and so on. You know who you are!

I'm eternally grateful to my awesome agent, Cyle Young, and my very patient editor, Ashley Runyon, for believing in a book about persimmons. So honored to work with both of you.

I want to thank my wonderful son-in-law Wes Hovious and my precious youngest daughter, Ally, for picking persimmons with me and allowing me to take pictures of the entire process. Love you both!

I couldn't have completed this book without the help of my amazing editorial intern, Megan Alms. She keeps me sane. I know I won't be able to keep her long—she's too gifted—but I am grateful for the work she did on this project.

I would like to thank my forever friend Angie McCullough for listening to me drone on and on about this book during our morning gym workouts and for helping me track down some great stories. Love you, Ang!

Special thanks to the folks at the Lawrence County Tourism Commission for all of their help. Y'all are the best!

I want to acknowledge my very supportive husband, Jeffrey. Whether I need help processing persimmons or a Polar Pop to get me through a tough deadline, I always know he will come through. You're my rock, Jeff. Love you more.

Finally, I want to thank God for allowing me to work in an industry I love. I am blessed.

the perfect

PERSIMMON

introduction

*P*eople in the Midwest—especially those living in southern Indiana—take their persimmons seriously. But if you were to talk to people in other states about the fruit, they'd probably ask, "What's a persimmon?"

This puckery little fruit, when ripe, is the perfect ingredient for amazing desserts, and you'll find lots of those in the following pages. One thing I discovered when researching for this book was that people are passionate about their persimmon recipes. Using cinnamon instead of allspice or replacing buttermilk with cream makes for a very different persimmon pudding. One pinch of this or another pinch of that can completely change the flavor. For that reason, I have included several variations of recipes for essentially the same dessert or dish. I encourage you to try all the variations and maybe even experiment with your own.

As you'll discover, there's more than one variety of persimmon, and different persimmons make very different dishes. For example, the persimmons found in the western part of the United States are bigger and different in texture, and they are perfect for salads and soups and many other side dishes. The common persimmon found in the Midwest is more suited for desserts. I've included recipes featuring both kinds of persimmons. However, full disclosure here: I'm more of a common persimmon person since that's what I grew up with and have loved ever since I was old enough to toddle around the Mitchell Persimmon Festival in Lawrence County, Indiana.

I have several plastic bags of persimmon pulp in my freezer right now, and you can bet I'll be experimenting with more persimmon-y creations in days to come. I hope you'll do the same. I also hope you'll enjoy the interesting, little-known facts and folklore surrounding persimmons and the people who love and celebrate them.

Last, I hope that if you're already a lover of persimmons, this book will speak your love language, possibly introduce you to new information surrounding persimmons, and offer new recipes. If you've never tried a persimmon before, I hope you'll be a bit adventurous and allow your taste buds to appreciate this lovely little fruit.

chapter one

THE HISTORY, THE
VARIETIES, THE LORE

I love persimmons. One taste of a ripe persimmon, and I'm transported to my growing up years in Southern Indiana. It wasn't a true family get-together or church pitch-in if somebody didn't bring the persimmon pudding. Once I learned how to make really amazing persimmon pudding, I was asked to bring it for dessert to every family reunion, birthday party, and holiday gathering. I knew I had really arrived when I was trusted with such an important task, so I have proudly carted my persimmon pudding to every family function since that day of persimmon pudding promotion.

It seems my family isn't alone in its affinity for persimmons. Even its name celebrates the fruit's yumminess. The American persimmon tree (*Diospyros virginiana*), which accounts for most of the persimmon trees in the Midwest, shares a scientific genus, *Diospyros*, with Asian persimmons. *Diospyros* means "divine fruit" or "fruit of the gods"[1]—which just about sums it up because persimmons are truly heavenly.

About the size of a plum, and orange in color when ripe, American persimmons are also called common persimmons. Of course in my family, we just call them delicious . . . but not until they're ripe. If you make the mistake of plucking an American persimmon from a tree while it's still green and bite

The American persimmon, up close and personal.

into it expecting a sweet sensation, you're in a for a taste experience you'll never forget, and I mean that in a "this is the most puckery, bitter fruit I've ever tasted in my life" kind of way. Or, as author Raymond Sokolov states in his book *Fading Feast*, quoting Captain John Smith, "If it not be ripe, it will drawe a man's mouth awrie with much torment."[2] Seriously, it takes just one bite into a green persimmon to scar a person for life. *Bitter* doesn't even begin to describe it!

Which reminds me of a joke I once heard. A man is seated next to a country music executive on an airplane. The two begin chatting, and the man says, "I've noticed that some of the biggest names in country music are losing their hair . . . and I have a solution for that."

The country music executive is intrigued and says, "Really? What's that?"

The man leans in and whispers, "Well, you get you a quart of alum juice and a quart of green persimmon juice and mix it all together. Then you massage that mixture on top of the bald head."

"And that works?" asks the music executive. "It grows hair on the head?"

"Naw," the man says, "but it'll draw their sideburns up on top of their head."

Ba dum dum.

Now that's sour! But, if you're patient and wait for the American persimmon to ripen and fall from the branches, it's one of the sweetest tastes ever.

THE VARIETIES

The American persimmon can withstand temperatures as low as twenty-five degrees below Fahrenheit and can be found as far south as Florida, as far north as Connecticut, as far west as Iowa, and even in some parts of Texas.[3] But if you were to

Here's a famous Lawrence County persimmon tree.
Photo by author.

ask anyone in my neck of the woods where the most perfect plethora of persimmons happened to be, they'd no doubt say, "Lawrence County, Indiana" or, more specifically, "Mitchell, Indiana," where you'll find a persimmon proudly painted on the town's water tower. Mitchell is also home to the Persimmon Festival, held there each year since 1946. (More on that famous festival in chapter 2.) Since I was born and raised in Lawrence County, Indiana, I would have to agree. We have many persimmon trees here, and some of the best, most creative cooks in all of the Midwest. (I'll be sharing some of those persimmon recipes in chapter 3.)

According to my local sources, not all American persimmon trees are created equal. It seems some trees just produce sweeter persimmons than others. No one quite knows the reason, but ask any local persimmon aficionado, and that person will know the location of the best persimmon trees—the ones that produce the sweetest fruit, year after year. Of course, those persimmon trees are not only highly regarded but also highly guarded—especially if it's close to the Annual Persimmon Pudding Contest that's part of the Lawrence County Persimmon Festival each autumn. So, if you're like me and have no persimmon trees on your property, you'd better cozy up to someone who does, or you can buy persimmon pulp from area farmers' markets.

Here are some additional basic facts about the American persimmon tree:

- American persimmons are much smaller than Asian persimmons.

- The American variety requires a long season to ripen. If you can press your thumb into it and it mashes down, then it's probably ripe enough to use in cooking. Or, just wait for the persimmon to fall to the ground.

- Unripe fruits are really astringent.

- Ripe fruits are extremely sweet and have a soft, jelly-like texture.

- The trees can grow fifty to seventy-five feet tall, but most are maintained at fifteen to thirty feet tall.

- They flower by late May.

- In most cases, they require both male and female plants to bear fruit.[4]

Honestly, until I started researching for this book, I had no idea there were different kinds of persimmons other than the ones grown in the Midwest or that persimmons could be used for anything besides desserts. I bet some of you are also having that same sort of epiphany right now.

Since I'm not a horticulturist, and because this is not a scientific journal, I'm not going to delve into the many variations

See how small they are? *Photo by author.*

of persimmons grown in the United States, but I think it is important to understand a couple of the major varieties and how they differ from one another. I already covered the American persimmon, so let's talk a bit about the Asian variety, *Diospyros kaki*. The Asian persimmon tree can survive temps that dip down to zero degrees Fahrenheit, and they are grown mostly in Southern and Central California as well as Arizona, Texas, Louisiana, and a few other southern states. Also commonly called Fuyu, the Asian persimmon is not to be confused with the seedless Hachiya persimmon, which also grows in the West. Though both are the same orange hue, the Fuyu is shaped like a tomato while the Hachiya resembles an acorn shape. But here's the biggest, most important difference: Fuyu persimmons are sweet all the time while Hachiya persimmons are very astringent until they are ripe.[5]

Here are some additional basic facts about the Asian persimmon tree:

Persimmons that have fallen to the ground are ripe enough to cook with. *Photo by author.*

- *o* Also known as the Fuyu persimmon, the tree's fruit is almost always sweet and can be eaten when firm.
- *o* The Asian species accounts for most of the commercial persimmon production.
- *o* You do not need to plant a male tree and a female tree to get fruit. It's a self-fertile species.
- *o* These trees live a long time and are fruitful after forty years or longer.
- *o* The Asian persimmon tree (also called the Kaki tree) didn't arrive in the United States until 1856.
- *o* It's a pretty tree, with its leaves turning a reddish-orange or deep gold in the fall. In the spring, it produces yellow flowers.
- *o* This persimmon tree grows to about thirty feet tall.[6]

THE HISTORY

As you might imagine, we Hoosiers are quite proud of our persimmon heritage, so we celebrate it, talk about it, and write about it. Fellow journalist and Lawrence County history buff L. Joyce Mundy recently shared a bit of persimmon history in our local newspaper, the *Bedford Times Mail*, noting that persimmons were quite important to our pioneer ancestors who first settled in southern Indiana in the early 1800s. These European settlers supplemented their diets of wild game and nuts with many fruits, including persimmons. They were smart to do so, as persimmons are a good source of vitamin A and antioxidants, and they taste pretty good, too.

Apparently persimmons were also a good source of sweetening for the hooch—persimmon wine and persimmon beer, to be exact. In fact, the pioneers used to call this beer "possum toddy" because opossums were often found under persimmon trees eating the fallen fruit.[7]

Did you know?

The persimmon tree has also been called possum wood because opossums love its fruit so much.

Though *persimmon* is an early colonial word, it comes from the Powhatan name for the fruit, *pichamin*. It seems many Native American tribes considered persimmons a favorite fruit. They ate them plain as well as cooked into puddings. The Algonquin Indians, who called persimmon *putchamin*, dried the fruit, while others used its bark and syrup for medicine, especially when treating mouth and throat illnesses.[8]

According to an article by Francis Skalicky in the *Springfield News-Leader*, Spanish explorer Hernando de Soto mentioned persimmons in his journal, calling them a tasty fruit and the source of a bread made by Native Americans.

THE LORE

The Native Americans gave us more than just the name *persimmon*. They also gave us a few legends revolving around this fabulous fruit. Here's one I found about the origin of the raccoon: The Great Spirit commissioned a man to take a journey at once. The Great Spirit told the man, "This is a journey of the spirit and not the body. You must not eat or drink until the task is completed." The man was not quite ready for such a spiritual journey, however, because when he came upon a grove of persimmon trees, he could see the fruit was perfect for eating. He could not resist the temptation, so he stopped and ate until he could eat no more.

That angered the Great Spirit. He said to the man, "You will spend the rest of your days scurrying around the earth as a small, furry creature." The man begged for forgiveness, but the Great Spirit remained firm in his decision and turned the man into a raccoon—an animal that leaves footprints like a human, uses its hands like a man, and has the keen ability to always know when the persimmons are just right for picking.[9]

Persimmon folklore isn't found only in Native American history but also in Korean mythology. Persimmons are thought to be a sort of protector from predators such as the tiger, which probably stems from the famous Korean tale "The Tiger and the Persimmon." Though there are many different versions of this story, the basic elements are the same in every retelling.

One night, in a small village, a tiger was stalking the perimeter, looking for a cow to devour. Little did he know, a burglar was also on the prowl, hoping to steal a cow for his own purposes. Meanwhile, a child was crying loudly in the village, and no matter how the nearby villagers tried to console the child, the crying continued.

The villagers, distracted by the baby's cries, failed to notice either the burglar or the tiger. The curious tiger drew nearer and nearer to the child, but the baby kept crying, even though the villagers pleaded with the child to stop. Finally, one woman had an idea.

"Here's a dried persimmon," she said to the child, and immediately the baby stopped its wailing.

This stopped the tiger in its tracks, worried he might encounter this scariest of things called a "persimmon" that had frightened the baby into silence. At the same moment, the burglar jumped right on top of the tiger, mistaking it for the cow, and in a state of great fear, the tiger bolted out of the village with the burglar riding his back. Surely, thought the tiger, the burglar had to be that "persimmon" that had so scared the child it stopped crying. So the tiger just kept on running.[10]

SEEDS MEET NEEDS

Another bit of folklore that many still embrace as absolute truth is the persimmon seed's ability to predict the coming winter weather. If the pattern inside a persimmon seed is a spoon shape, that means there will be lots of heavy snow to shovel; a fork pattern indicates the winter will be mild, with dustings of powdery snow; and a knife shape means the winter will be very cold, with cutting winds.

Now, I'd heard about the persimmon seed's weather-predicting superpower for years, but I'd never cut open a seed myself until I was researching for this book. After gathering many ripe persimmons from a lovely tree in Springville, Indiana, in September, I hurried home to begin the process of straining the

The spoon shape inside persimmon seeds. *Photo by author.*

pulp from my find. But first, I took several persimmon seeds and sliced them open. Guess what I found? Spoons. All spoons. So, I have a snow shovel and salt on standby in my garage. Of course, I may not need them because, after much research, I've found that weather experts say the persimmon seed prediction is accurate only about 25 percent of the time.

Persimmon seeds have been used for many things besides forecasting the weather. During the Civil War, mostly in the South, people substituted persimmon seeds for buttons. Persimmon seeds were also used to make coffee. You see, the Union blockade of Confederate port cities kept coffee from making its way down south, so the Southerners had to figure

Did you know?
Persimmon wood is often used in making golf clubs.

out a way to survive without that precious commodity. You've heard the saying "necessity is the mother of invention"? Well, it's true. An 1863 edition of the *Montgomery Advertiser* (Alabama) printed, "The seeds of the persimmon when roasted and ground produces a beverage which cannot, even by old and experienced coffee drinkers, be distinguished from genuine coffee."[11] From food to medicine to alcoholic beverages to buttons to coffee—the persimmon and its seeds have been blessing us for centuries.

chapter Two

A TALE OF TWO FESTIVALS

*T*he Mitchell Persimmon Festival in Lawrence County, Indiana, is one of the oldest and longest running festivals in the state of Indiana. Most festivals run two or three days, but the Mitchell Persimmon Festival runs seven days, Saturday to Saturday (no activities on Sunday), in mid- to late September. It truly is the best of food, folks, and fun—especially if you're hankering for some of the tastiest persimmon pudding in the world. The Mitchell Persimmon Festival has been a popular event since the late 1940s. The city of Mitchell is already gearing up for the seventy-fifth annual Persimmon Festival in 2021—so you know it's going to be good!

Sure, the midway rides, the food booths, the cornhole tournament, the motorcycle show, the nightly musical events, the persimmon 5K race, the photo contest, the grand parade, the Persimmon Idol singing contest, and the crowning of the Persimmon Festival queen are all well-attended events. But the heart of the Persimmon Festival, the event that brings Lawrence Countians back home every September, is the persimmon pudding and persimmon novelty dessert contests. Every novice baker longs to have his or her name placed in the prestigious listing of persimmon pudding winners dating back to 1947. And 2018's persimmon pudding contest offered

A newspaper clipping from Lawrence County's own Persimmon Festival. *Photo by author.*

not only bragging rights but also a hefty $1,000 award for first prize. That year, Gary Rayhill Jr. beat out more than 180 persimmon pudding bakers to snag the prize money, and Trudy Dillman walked away with $100 for earning first place in the persimmon novelty dessert contest. (You'll find a few of the past award-winning recipes in chapter 3.)

The Mitchell Persimmon Festival kicks off with a candlelight tour at Spring Mill State Park's Pioneer Village. As the name hints, this village was a working, thriving pioneer village from 1814 to the late 1880s, and every year during the candlelight tour, it becomes active once again. Hundreds of volunteers dress in period attire and reenact what life might have been like during that time in that village, and between six thousand and eight thousand people attend this five-hour event. It's always a great way to kick off the Persimmon Festival.

Persimmon baking contest winners of the 2011 Persimmon Festival.
Photo courtesy of Lawrence County Tourism Commission.

Unless you've actually experienced the Persimmon Festival, it's tough to put into words the charm, heart, and absolute Hoosier hospitality you'll encounter during the week of events. Local folks grow up going to the festival every single year. As children, they enjoy the rides, the various Persimmon Festival little miss and queen competitions, and, of course, the parade that boasts more than 150 units. As adults, Lawrence Countians participate in events like the 5k walk/run and the persimmon pudding contest. Even people who grow up and move away from the persimmon capital of the world often return for at least part of the Persimmon Festival each year.

Enjoying the persimmon carousel has been a tradition for generations. *Photo by Pete Schreiner, the* Bedford Times-Mail, *provided by Lawrence County Tourism Commission.*

Honored guests on the Mitchell Chamber of Commerce parade float. *Photo courtesy of Lawrence County Tourism Commission.*

The persimmon queen and her court in the Persimmon Festival parade.
Photo courtesy of Lawrence County Tourism Commission.

In fact, according to the Lawrence County, Indiana, visitor guide, more than thirty thousand visitors attend the festival each year. Considering the City of Mitchell is home to only 4,300 residents, that's a lot of traffic, and for good reason. It's an amazing week jam-packed with everything a festival should be—Americana at its best. In fact, Mitchell is gaining even more national recognition for its Persimmon Festival. It was just named Best Food Festival in the great state of Indiana

Did you know?
Some say persimmons
taste a lot like pumpkins.

by *National Geographic*.[1] You might want to check it out for yourself. But if you can't make your way to southern Indiana to devour a piece of prize-winning persimmon pudding in September, I have backup plans for you: Year round, you can pop into the Millstone Dining Room at Spring Mill Inn in Mitchell, Indiana, and order a piece of persimmon pudding. (Locals rave

About thirty thousand people attend the Persimmon Festival each year. *Photo courtesy of Lawrence County Tourism Commission.*

about it!) Also, Mitchell's Huckleberry Bakery offers lots of persimmon treats, such as persimmon slushies, and Applacres on Highway 37 sells frozen persimmon pulp so you can make some of the recipes in this book.

The Mitchell Persimmon Festival may be the oldest persimmon festival, but it's certainly not the only one. Colfax,

Even the Mitchell water tower pays tribute to the persimmon!
Photo by Kaydy Miller.

North Carolina, is home to the Colfax Persimmon Festival, which celebrated its eleventh anniversary in November 2018. Founder Gene Stafford began the festival on his family farm for several reasons, according to information on the festival's website (www.colfaxpersimmonfest.com). Stafford's farm dates back to pre-Revolutionary War days. And not only is it historic, it is also plentiful with persimmons! Stafford desired to find a way to celebrate the persimmon harvest, promote local artisans, and showcase country traditions as well as raise a little money to renovate and save the family farm.

The result? The inaugural one-day Colfax Persimmon Festival on the Stafford Farm in 2008. About one thousand people visited the fourteen-acre farm that first year. In 2009, the festival drew close to two thousand visitors, and it continues flourishing and growing. If you plan to go in November, you'll experience live music and arts and crafts, and you'll also be able to buy lots of persimmon-y items. Yay!

Speaking of persimmons and November, there's another persimmon party happening on the third Sunday in November in Old Towne in Orange, California—at least it happens most years. It's been canceled at least once due to drought and a low-yield persimmon season. But most years you can enjoy a day of music, unique persimmon concoctions, and lots of fun at Old Towne's celebrated Pitcher Park—and all proceeds benefit the preservation of this charming historic pocket park.

About two hundred folks come out for this persimmon party each year, and they have Russ and Patricia Barrios to thank for it. According to a story in the *Orange County Register*, this lovely couple began the event in 1995 to keep the persimmon history of the area alive. Persimmon trees were quite popular in Orange in the 1920s and the 1930s, having been brought to the area from Japan, and many persimmon trees remain.

chapter three

THE RECIPES

THE PROCESS OF PERSIMMON PULP

Before I share all of these scrumptious persimmon recipes, there's one secret you need to know—how to get that precious persimmon pulp from the fruit. Fuyu persimmons make a delicious pulp that's much like the consistency of applesauce, and if you can't buy it at your local farmers' market or beg your relatives to share their persimmon pulp stash, you'd better learn to produce your own pulp.

Here's a simple slow cooker recipe for extracting that precious pulp: All you'll need is enough Fuyu persimmons to fill a slow cooker and about 5 cups of water. You can also add 2 tablespoons of ground cinnamon for a little extra flavor, if you like. Start by cleaning and cutting your persimmons. When you cut them, you'll want to cut off the stem end, then cut the fruit into quarter slices. No need to peel them—the skin will come off later in the process. (And it's totally safe to eat.) Then put the water, the optional cinnamon, and your persimmons into the slow cooker. Put the lid on and cook everything overnight (8 to 10 hours). When you come back to them, they should be looking more brownish in color.

After they're done cooking, put a small portion of your persimmons into a sieve. Hold the sieve over a large pot and mash the persimmons through the holes, letting the mashed fruit fall into the pot. This will filter out the skin and squish the fruit into an applesauce-like consistency. Repeat this process with small portions of your persimmons until you've emptied the slow cooker.

Now, for the common persimmons—the ones we have growing wild in Indiana. You'll usually have to wait to gather them until after the first hard frost, but you'll know when they are ripe because they'll become soft and fall to the ground. In fact, some folks who have persimmon trees on their property will place a tarp underneath their trees to catch the ripened persimmons. You'll have to be quick to gather the fruit because deer and raccoons also love persimmons. After gathering them, place the persimmons in a bowl of water and then drain that water, just to remove any dirt or debris.

To make persimmon pulp, you'll first have to remove the caps of the persimmons and discard them. Next, place the persimmons in the strainer or sieve with a bowl underneath, and begin mashing the persimmons. (This can take a while, but your efforts will be rewarded when you bake that first persimmon pudding of the season.) As you mash, the seeds will remain behind, and the sweet persimmon pulp will end up in your bowl. You can also use a food mill to accomplish this, but I find you waste more of the persimmon pulp that way. Next, divide your pulp into 2-cup servings and place into separate freezer bags. (We separate into 2-cup batches because most recipes call for 2 cups of pulp.) Freeze the precious pulp until you're ready to use . . . and that's it! It's that easy. Now, you're ready to tackle the recipes in this book. I recommend starting with my late mother-in-law's persimmon pudding . . . but I might be biased.

Mashing the persimmons into a sieve.
Photo by author.

DESSERTS

I wasn't aware that persimmon pudding was a "Midwestern best kept secret" until we moved to Texas for a ten-year stint, and I was no longer able to buy persimmon pulp. I used to crave persimmon pudding so much that I'd have my mother-in-law, Martha Davis, ship me frozen persimmon pulp all the way from Indiana so I could make my favorite pudding in my Texas kitchen, miles away from my beloved Hoosier roots. But now that we've moved back to southern Indiana, I am once again in persimmon pudding paradise, so I thought I'd share my mother-in-law's pudding recipe with you.

You know how they say, "The way to a man's heart is through his stomach"? Well, persimmon pudding is definitely the pathway to my hubby's heart, so I'm eternally grateful that my late mom-in-law shared her recipe with me.

We like it served cold, with whipped topping. However, some prefer to spoon the optional sauce over the top and serve it that way. Either way, trust me—you're going to love it!

Finished persimmon pulp, all mashed-up and ready to cook with.
Photo by author.

Persimmon pulp all bagged up and ready to freeze. *Photo by author.*

Martha's Practically Perfect Persimmon Pudding

INGREDIENTS

5 tablespoons butter

1 cup sugar

½ cup firmly packed brown sugar

2 eggs

1½ cups flour

1 teaspoon cinnamon

¼ teaspoon allspice

1 teaspoon baking powder

¼ teaspoon baking soda

¼ teaspoon salt

1½ cups milk

1½ cups persimmon pulp

OPTIONAL SAUCE

1 cup brown sugar

2 tablespoons cornstarch

1 teaspoon cinnamon

½ teaspoon allspice

1 tablespoon butter

1 cup water

DIRECTIONS

For the pudding, cream the butter, sugars, and eggs together. Mix the flour, cinnamon, allspice, baking powder, baking soda, and salt together in a separate bowl. Add the dry ingredients to the butter and sugar mixture a little at a time until blended. Stir in the milk and persimmon pulp. Grease a 9-by-13-inch glass pan and pour in the persimmon pudding mixture. Bake at 350 degrees until the sides pull away from the pan (approximately 45 to 50 minutes—but be sure to check frequently to avoid overbaking). Let your persimmon pudding cool, and cover with plastic wrap. Lastly, place it in the fridge to chill.

For the optional sauce, combine all ingredients in a medium saucepan and cook over medium to high heat until the mixture is the consistency of gravy. Spoon onto the pudding as desired.

Fresh from the oven, here's a pan of persimmon pudding I made. See how it pulls away from the sides of the glass pan? That's how you know it's done. *Photo by author.*

Served cold and with whipped topping, persimmon pudding is a crowd pleaser. No family get-together is complete if someone doesn't show up with a pan of persimmon pudding. *Photo by author.*

Daddy Bob's Persimmon Pudding

It seems every family has its tried-and-true persimmon pudding recipe, and though it may differ by only one-half of a teaspoon of cinnamon or 1 cup of milk instead of 1 cup of cream, those small adjustments make a huge difference in taste and texture. For that reason, I'm going to include several different persimmon pudding recipes throughout this book, so that you can decide which version is your family's favorite.

This one comes from my dear friend JoniSue Ryan. She said, "My sweet stepdad made this for us when I was growing up and until he passed to heaven. He loved to cook and bake."

INGREDIENTS

1 stick butter

2 cups persimmon pulp

¾ cup white sugar

¾ cup light brown sugar

⅛ teaspoon salt

1 teaspoon baking soda

1 teaspoon baking powder

1½ cups flour

2 eggs

1½ cups milk or buttermilk

1 teaspoon pure vanilla

1 teaspoon cinnamon

DIRECTIONS

Preheat oven to 325 degrees and melt one stick of butter in a large oblong pan. (The Le Creuset 6-by-10-inch baking pan is the perfect size.) Mix pulp and sugars in a large mixing bowl. In a separate bowl, mix the salt, baking soda, baking powder, and flour. Gradually stir the dry ingredients into the pulp mixture, adding a bit at a time. Then add the eggs, milk, vanilla, and cinnamon, and stir everything together. Pour the mixture into the preheated pan with the melted butter (it makes the edges nice and crispy), and bake 45 to 50 minutes. The pudding is done when it pulls away from the sides of the pan, or when you can insert a toothpick into the center of the pudding and it comes out without any residue. Let cool and serve with whipped topping.

Grandma Kettrey's Persimmon Pudding

Rosita Voorhies looks forward to autumns in Indiana because that means she'll be able to make her Grandma Kettrey's Persimmon Pudding. And she goes about it the same way her grandma did—she gathers persimmons from a neighbor's 40-year-old persimmon tree, and she processes those persimmons wearing her Grandma Kettrey's apron. But you don't have to have Grandma Kettrey's apron to make her amazing pudding. So go for it!

INGREDIENTS

2 cups persimmon pulp

2 cups white sugar

2 eggs

2 teaspoons baking soda

1½ cups buttermilk

1½ cups flour

⅛ teaspoon salt

1 teaspoon baking powder

1 teaspoon cinnamon

¼ cup half-and-half

¼ cup melted butter

BUTTER GLAZE SAUCE

½ cup sugar

1 tablespoon flour

¼ cup water

¼ cup half-and-half

2 tablespoons butter

1 teaspoon vanilla

DIRECTIONS

For the pudding, cream the pulp, sugar, and eggs together in a large bowl. Add the baking soda to the buttermilk in a liquid measuring cup and stir together. Allow extra room as it will foam. In another bowl, whisk together the flour, salt, baking powder, and cinnamon. Stir half the dry ingredient mixture into the pulp mixture. Stir in half the buttermilk. Repeat with the remaining dry ingredients and buttermilk. Next, stir in the half-and-half and melted butter. Spread into a well-greased 13-by-9-inch pan and bake for about 60 minutes at 325 degrees. The pudding is done when it pulls away from the

Balls of cookie dough ready to bake. *Photo by author.*

sides of the pan, or when you can insert a toothpick into the center of the pudding and it comes out without any residue. Cool.

After the pudding has cooled, make the sauce. Begin by mixing together the sugar, flour, and water. Cook until it thickens and then add the half-and-half, butter, and vanilla. Bring to a boil.

Pour the sauce over the cooled persimmon pudding and enjoy.

The perfect batter consistency. *Photo by author.*

*W*hen I met my writer friend Bobbie Frazier of North Carolina, we discovered we had a lot in common— including our love of persimmons. When she said, "In the South, we refer to persimmons as a delicacy," I knew I'd met a kindred spirit.

When Bobbie wrote the following story and said I could use it for my book, I was thrilled. She has also provided us with her prize-winning persimmon pudding recipe.

———

"Is this what you call a persimmon?" my father, Herb, asked his soon-to-be bride, my mother, Mary, as he popped a green persimmon in his mouth.

Anyone who knows anything about persimmons knows that is the very worst thing you could do with a green persimmon. Before mom could stop him, there it was, sitting in his mouth, holding his teeth apart. The persimmon was so astringent that he couldn't close his mouth around it. It was a puckery predicament for sure!

Now, I, their daughter, sixty-five years later, pick persimmons from that same tree and make award-winning persimmon puddings with those squishy little gems. Here in the South, persimmon pudding is a delicacy, with hundreds of different ways to make it. However, according to my husband, there is only one correct recipe—mine!

The joke is that we couldn't marry before I had mastered making his mom's persimmon pudding and pumpkin pie. Chuckling, he often tells people, "It was a premarital agreement."

His mother spent many hours teaching me how to make the perfect pudding. From collecting the fruit, to getting the pulp, to dividing and freezing the pulp, to creating the pudding—I learned it all. I have changed it a bit over the years, with my husband's approval as well as his two brothers' blessings, since it is a staple at our home during the Thanksgiving and Christmas holidays. And when we have out-of-town visitors, I usually make a persimmon pudding because either they've never tried it, or they have tried it and they're coming back for more.

The texture of persimmon pudding is different, almost like a dense cake that has not cooked long enough—or like a brownie. Many people have a preconceived notion of what it will taste like, so when they scoop up a tidbit on their fork, just enough to satisfy the hostess, it is a guessing game. Will they like it or not? But when they come back for a second piece, that tells me they have become persimmon pudding believers.

Of course, in order to make persimmon pudding for family and those newly converted persimmon believers, you have to have pulp on hand. So in our home, the persimmon pudding space in the freezer is precious, like the safe for the gold at Fort Knox.

Mabel's Persimmon Pudding

INGREDIENTS

1 stick margarine, softened

2 cups white sugar

2 eggs

2 cups persimmon pulp

2 cups self-rising flour

2 cups milk

1 teaspoon vanilla

DIRECTIONS

In a mixing bowl, mix the margarine, sugar, and eggs by hand. Add the 2 cups persimmon pulp and stir. Then alternate adding some self-rising flour and some milk, mixing well after each addition, until all the flour and *most* of the milk are incorporated. The consistency should be almost like cake batter. If it seems too thick, add a little more milk at the end. Add in the vanilla. Pour the mixture into a 9-by-12-inch or 9-by-13-inch baking dish. Bake at 350 degrees for 60 minutes, or maybe a little longer. When the pudding becomes more golden in color and begins pulling away from the sides of the pan, it's done. To be really sure, insert a toothpick into the center of the pudding, and if it comes out pudding free, you know it's done.

When Treva Olson of Lawrence County, Indiana, was teaching Public Speaking and Composition at Mitchell (Indiana) High School, she not only taught her students important lessons but also took time to educate a fellow teacher who'd moved to Lawrence County from Chicago about the county's beloved Persimmon Festival.

"I just don't get all of this fuss," the Chicagoan said, referring to the many Airstream campers flooding the city for the annual festival. Treva shared a bit about the history of the festival and her love for persimmon pulp.

"Around here we use persimmon pulp to make cookies, pudding, and bread," Treva said. "I actually like to eat the raw persimmon pulp."

"Really?" the northerner inquired. Several days later, the Chicagoan greeted Treva in the teachers' lounge and said, "You all may think this persimmon stuff is wonderful, but I made a persimmon pudding, and it was horrible."

Treva was puzzled, but as her fellow teacher continued her persimmon rant, the mystery was solved. Apparently, no one had told the new Lawrence Countian that the persimmons have to ripen, meaning they need to be orange and squishy—not green—when making a persimmon pudding.

Looking back on that funny memory, Treva joked, "I'm surprised her family didn't die . . . deer may eat the green persimmons, but they aren't fit for humans."

So, for all of you northerners, or anyone who is not acquainted with persimmons, take note—ripe persimmons are sweet; green ones are bitter.

During our chat about the Chicago teacher making persimmon pudding out of green persimmons, Treva shared that she is quite fond of raw persimmon pudding, so in her honor, I share her recipe, which is also a favorite in our family.

Treva's Raw Persimmon Pudding

INGREDIENTS

1 cup sugar

1 cup persimmon pulp

1 cup miniature marshmallows

1 cup pecans, chopped

2½ cups graham cracker crumbs
  (may take more)

Powdered sugar (as needed)

Whipped cream (as needed)

DIRECTIONS

Mix sugar, pulp, marshmallows, and nuts together thoroughly. Keep adding graham cracker crumbs until the dough is stiff enough to roll out and shape like a jelly roll. Sprinkle powdered sugar onto a sheet of waxed paper and roll the dough into the powdered sugar until it is covered thoroughly. Roll the persimmon dough up in the waxed paper. Twist the ends of the waxed paper and place in the fridge to chill for at least 12 hours. Slice like a jelly roll and serve with a dollop of real whipped cream.

Persimmon Spice and Everything Nice Cookies

My lovely college friend Sylvia Boykin Neff shared this persimmon cookie recipe with me. She says many variations of this recipe exist, in some of which you're encouraged to add raisins, cranberries, nuts, and even chocolate chips, but she's a purist, stating, "I have always preferred them plain." I'm with her, but don't take our word for it. Experiment with the different variations.

INGREDIENTS

1 cup very ripe persimmon pulp

½ teaspoon baking soda

½ cup unsalted butter (4 ounces or 1 stick) at room temperature

½ cup granulated sugar

½ cup brown sugar

1 egg

1 teaspoon pure vanilla extract

1 teaspoon grated orange zest

2 cups flour

2 teaspoons baking powder

1 teaspoon ground cinnamon

¼ teaspoon ground cloves

½ teaspoon salt

DIRECTIONS

Puree the ripe persimmon pulp until smooth. Stir in the baking soda. Beat together the butter and sugars in a large bowl. Beat in the egg and vanilla extract. Mix in the persimmon puree and orange zest. In a separate bowl, whisk the flour, baking powder, cinnamon, ground cloves, and salt. Next, add the dry ingredients little by little into the persimmon mixture. Cover the mixture and chill for about an hour. Lastly, drop by teaspoons onto a greased cookie sheet and bake at 350 degrees for approximately 12 to 15 minutes or until the cookies are brown around the edges.

The perfect persimmon cookie—with a big bite taken out of it! *Photo by author.*

We added icing on top of our cookies. Yum! *Photo by author.*

I love soft serve persimmon ice cream, but I don't always have time to make it. We frequently visit this Jiffy Treet in Bedford, Indiana, during September and October in order to score some persimmon ice cream while it's still available. *Photo by author.*

!NOW SERVING!
!~ FAMOUS~!
SOFT PERSIMMON

Chicken Strip Sandwich..............
Chicken Nuggets ....
Chicken Breast Strips.....................
Grilled Chicken Breast Sandwich........................
Breaded Chicken Sandwich ....
Chicken Club............................
Chicken Wrap ....

SALADS

Garden Salad ....
(crisp lettuce, carrots, green peppers, radishes, tomatoes)

Chef Salad........................
(crisp lettuce, ham, carrots, green peppers, radishes, tomatoes, chec

Jiffy Treet's soft serve persimmon ice cream is a crowd pleaser in Bedford, Indiana. *Photo by author.*

While Mary A. Michael was visiting her new sister-in-law, Kaye, in Springville, Indiana, in 1962, she encountered a new dessert. "Though I was a little reluctant to try it, she encouraged me to do so," Mary said. "And, boy was I surprised by its delicate and unusual taste!"

From that point on, Mary became a hunter of persimmon trees. "I learned to spot a tree and not be embarrassed to ask a stranger if she would share or even sell the magnificent fruit to me," Mary said. "I also learned while camping at McCormick's

Creek with my new in-laws that humans are not the only ones who love persimmons. You have to get them before the raccoons do! They are big fans!"

Over the years, Mary has improvised, created, and perfected many recipes of her own, including recipes starring the fruit she fell in love with back in 1962. Of all things persimmon, these cookies are her favorite. "The cookies make lovely gifts for Christmas, and I have so enjoyed sending them to my brother in Florida each year," she said. "As my ninetieth birthday approaches this week, I am thankful to God for blessing me with the gift of cooking and baking for my family and friends. I hope you enjoy my recipe, and I wish you luck and happy hunting for the perfect persimmons!"

Oh, and one more thing Mary added: "Don't be fooled by the store brand persimmon-flavored cookies."

This recipe makes about two dozen cookies, but they'll go fast, so consider doubling.

Mother Mary's Persimmon Cookies

INGREDIENTS

1 cup soft margarine	2 cups flour
1 cup sugar	1 teaspoon baking soda
1 cup persimmon pulp	½ teaspoon cinnamon
1 egg	1 cup raisins

DIRECTIONS

Cream together the margarine and sugar. Stir in the persimmon pulp and egg. Add the flour, soda, and cinnamon. Blend. Stir in the raisins. Drop by teaspoons onto an ungreased cookie sheet. Bake for 10 minutes at 350 degrees. Serve with a hot cup of Earl Grey and a dash of love from the persimmon trees of southern Indiana. Yields 24 cookies.

Chocolate Chip Persimmon Oatmeal Cookies

Here's another persimmon cookie recipe to try. My daughters adore this one because there are so many yummy ingredients—chocolate chips, persimmons, oatmeal—and it's so good!

INGREDIENTS

1½ cup persimmon pulp

1 cup butter, softened

2 eggs

1 cup sugar

1 cup light brown sugar

3 tablespoons milk

2 teaspoons vanilla extract

1½ cup flour

1 teaspoon salt

1 teaspoon baking soda

1 cup chocolate chips

2 cups rolled oats

DIRECTIONS

Puree the ripe persimmon pulp until smooth. In a large mixing bowl, blend the softened butter, eggs, sugars, milk, and vanilla extract. In a separate bowl, mix the flour, salt, and baking soda, then add the mixture to the batter. Next stir in the chocolate chips, oats, and persimmon puree. Grease a cookie sheet and drop the dough onto it by teaspoons. Bake for 8 to 10 minutes at 375 degrees. Yields 25 cookies.

Judy Shaw's Persimmon Pudding

If you're going to make a persimmon dessert, it might as well be an award-winning recipe, right? Well, you're in luck. Judy Shaw, whose recipe won the 2017 Mitchell Persimmon Festival pudding contest, shared her recipe in the 72nd Persimmon Festival official booklet, as did Akaylea Kirkman, whose persimmon torte also took home honors.

INGREDIENTS

2 cups persimmon pulp

3 eggs

2 cups sugar

1½ cups buttermilk

1 teaspoon baking soda

1½ cups flour

1 teaspoon baking powder

¼ teaspoon salt

¼ teaspoon cinnamon

¼ cup cream, half-and-half, or milk

½ stick margarine or butter, melted

¼ teaspoon vanilla

DIRECTIONS

Combine the pulp, eggs, and sugar. In a separate bowl, combine the buttermilk and baking soda, mixing until it foams a little. Stir into the pulp mixture. Sift together the flour, baking powder, salt, and cinnamon. Alternately add some of the dry ingredients and some of the milk to the persimmon mixture until all are incorporated. Stir in the butter and vanilla. Coat a 9-by-13-inch baking dish or two 8-by-8-inch baking dishes with grease or butter. Pour the batter into the greased dish. Bake for 45 minutes to one hour. When the pudding becomes more golden in color and begins pulling away from the sides of the pan, it's done. To be really sure, insert a toothpick into the center of the pudding, and if it comes out pudding free, you know it's done.

Persimmon Torte

FIRST LAYER

1 box French vanilla cake mix

½ cup water

½ cup persimmon pulp

⅓ cup vegetable oil

3 eggs

SECOND LAYER

1 large box of instant vanilla
    pudding mix

2 cups milk

½ cup persimmon pulp

TOPPING

1 (16-ounce) package Cool Whip

1 tub vanilla icing

¼ cup persimmon pulp

chopped nuts, to taste

DIRECTIONS

In a large bowl, mix together the cake mix, water, persimmon pulp, vegetable oil, and eggs. Pour the batter into a 9-by-13-inch baking dish. In a second bowl, mix the vanilla pudding mix, milk, and persimmon pulp until well blended. Spoon second layer over batter and bake at 350 degrees for 35 to 40 minutes or until it pulls away from the pan. Let cool.

For the icing, stir together the Cool Whip, icing, and persimmon pulp. Spread over the cooled cake and sprinkle with the chopped nuts. Refrigerate.

Persimmon Pie

When Mary Elizabeth (Simmerman) Parsley passed away at age ninety, her grandson, Adam Parsley, inherited her recipe box. And if that wasn't special enough, each recipe is recorded in her lovely cursive writing. Inside the treasure box, he found recipes for persimmon pie, persimmon cake, and the persimmon pudding that she claimed was the 1962 winner of the Persimmon Festival pudding contest. (However, according to the 72nd Annual Persimmon Festival guidebook, the 1962 winner was Mrs. Robert Cooper.) Adam was kind enough to share his grandmother's three treasured persimmon recipes with us.

INGREDIENTS

2 eggs, separated

1 cup persimmon pulp

1 tablespoon lemon juice

½ cup sugar

¼ teaspoon cinnamon

1 unbaked pie shell

DIRECTIONS

Beat the egg yolks. In a large bowl, combine the persimmon pulp, lemon juice, sugar, cinnamon, and egg yolks. Beat the egg whites and fold into the persimmon mixture. Pour the mixture into the unbaked pie shell and bake until firm, 40 to 45 minutes. Top with meringue or whipped cream.

1962 Award-Winning Persimmon Pudding

INGREDIENTS

2 cups persimmon pulp

2 large eggs

½ stick butter, softened

2 cups sugar

1⅓ cups buttermilk

1 teaspoon baking soda

1½ cups flour

1 teaspoon baking powder

⅛ teaspoon salt

DIRECTIONS

In a large mixing bowl, combine the persimmon pulp, eggs, butter, and sugar. Add the buttermilk and baking soda. Mix well. Sift the flour, baking powder, and salt, and stir this mixture into the persimmon mixture. The dough will be thin, but don't add more flour. Bake for 45 minutes at 350 degrees. If the corners are browning too quickly, turn the oven temperature down to 325 degrees.

Persimmon Cake

While some people love the flavor of persimmons, they are not fond of the texture of the famed persimmon pudding. (My daughter Abby falls into that category.) That's where this persimmon cake comes into play. It has all the persimmon flavor coupled with the familiar texture of cake.

INGREDIENTS

½ cup shortening

1½ cup sugar

2 eggs, beaten

2 cups self-rising flour

½ teaspoon baking soda

½ teaspoon cinnamon

½ teaspoon cloves

1 cup persimmon pulp

1 cup raisins (optional)

½ cup chopped nuts (optional)

ICING

2 tablespoons butter

½ cup brown sugar

½ cup milk

1½ cup powdered sugar

½ teaspoon vanilla

¼ teaspoon salt

DIRECTIONS

For the cake, lightly cream the shortening and sugar. Add the eggs and beat well. Sift together the flour, baking soda, cinnamon, and cloves. Add the sifted dry ingredients and the pulp to the shortening mixture and beat until smooth. Fold in the raisins and/or nuts. Bake in a 9-by-13-inch greased and floured pan. Bake at 350 degrees for 40 minutes or until the cake has a golden color and pulls away from the sides of the pan. Cool.

For the icing, melt the butter and add the brown sugar and milk. Bring to a boil; cook for 2 minutes. Then, remove from the heat and cool. Next, beat in the powdered sugar, vanilla, and salt. Spread the icing on the cooled cake.

Apple Streusel Persimmon Cake

INGREDIENTS

3 tablespoons butter

4 cups chopped apples

4 tablespoons sugar

1 teaspoon cinnamon

2 cups flour

1 teaspoon baking soda

½ teaspoon baking powder

1 cup brown sugar

1 stick butter, softened

¼ teaspoon salt

1 cup persimmon pulp

¼ cup sour cream

½ cup sugar

2 teaspoons ginger

2 large eggs

⅓ cup chopped crystallized ginger

DIRECTIONS

In a large skillet, melt the butter over medium heat. Next, add the apples and sauté for about 5 minutes. Add the sugar and cinnamon and sauté for 5 minutes more. Cool.

Grease a 9-by-9-inch cake pan. Preheat the oven to 350 degrees. In a large bowl, mix together the flour, baking soda, baking powder, brown sugar, butter, and salt. The mixture should be crumbly. Set aside ¾ cup of the mixture for topping. Puree the ripe persimmon pulp until smooth. Add the persimmon puree, sour cream, sugar, and ginger to the remaining flour mixture. Beat until smooth. Add in the eggs and stir. Pour the batter into the pan and place the apples on top. Sprinkle the crystallized ginger over the apples. Last, sprinkle the reserved topping mixture over the apples. Bake for 45 minutes or until the top is golden brown.

Cherry Chocolate Persimmon Cake

Any chocoholics in the house? This cake might be your favorite thing in the whole book. The rich chocolate flavor is balanced by the sweetness of the cherries and persimmons. It's the perfect combination.

INGREDIENTS

2½ cup all-purpose flour

1½ teaspoons baking soda

2½ teaspoons baking powder

1 teaspoon salt

½ cup cocoa powder

3 eggs, beaten

1 cup butter, melted

2 cups sugar

2 cups persimmons pulp

1 cup chopped nuts

1 (21-ounce) can cherry pie
   filling

DIRECTIONS

Preheat the oven to 350 degrees. Grease a 12-cup Bundt pan and dust with flour. In a bowl mix together the flour, baking soda, baking powder, salt, and cocoa. In another bowl, mix together the eggs, butter, sugar, and persimmon pulp. Beat well. Mix in the dry ingredients. Add the nuts and cherries and pour into the bunt pan. Bake for 50 minutes or until the cake appears springy, and set aside to cool. Tap the Bundt cake to loosen it from the pan. Add your favorite icing.

Pretty Persimmon Ice Cream

I like the food I'm serving to be pretty if at all possible. How about you? Well, persimmon ice cream is one of those desserts that is actually pretty while being pretty tasty, too. And, here's a shortcut you can take and still make a gorgeous dessert. Use a quart of softened vanilla ice cream—it doesn't even have to be homemade. I won't tell!

If you just don't want to make your own persimmon ice cream, I pray you have a Jiffy Treet near your house that serves this delicacy every autumn. We do, praise the Lord!

INGREDIENTS

2 cups persimmon pulp

2 tablespoons lemon juice

¼ teaspoon lemon zest

1 quart softened vanilla ice cream

DIRECTIONS

In a large bowl, mix together the persimmon pulp, lemon juice, and lemon zest. Add the quart of softened vanilla ice cream and mix until well blended. Pour the mixture into a freezer-safe container, cover, and freeze. Before serving, allow the mixture to thaw at room temperate for about 10 minutes. For a real kick, plop a scoop of this ice cream on top of a piece of persimmon pudding.

I like my persimmon ice cream without any toppings, but it's also yummy served with whipped cream and nuts! *Photo by author*.

Persimmon Festival Winner's Persimmon Ice Cream Dessert

Shared on LimestoneCountry.com, which promotes Lawrence County and all its uniqueness, this Persimmon Festival award-winning ice cream dessert will be a crowd pleaser. Enjoy!

INGREDIENTS

1 box caramel ice cream sandwiches

1 package golden sandwich cookies, crushed

1½ cups persimmon pulp

½ teaspoon cinnamon

2 (8-ounce) containers of whipped topping

Caramel sauce

1 cup chopped nuts

DIRECTIONS

Make a layer of ice cream sandwiches in a 9-by-13 pan. Mix the crushed cookies, persimmon pulp, cinnamon, and one container of whipped topping. Spread the mixture over the ice cream sandwiches. Spread the second container of whipped topping over the mixture. Drizzle with caramel sauce and sprinkle with chopped nuts. Freeze at least 12 hours before serving.

Yummy Persimmon Sorbet

Maybe you prefer a sorbet instead of ice cream. If that's the case, you'll love this recipe.

INGREDIENTS

4 to 5 large persimmons, peeled and chopped

¾ cup sugar

1 teaspoon fresh juice from 1 orange

½ teaspoon kosher salt

DIRECTIONS

Mix the persimmons and sugar in a blender. Process until smooth and well combined, then pour through a strainer. Whisk the orange juice and salt into 2 cups of the persimmons and sugar mixture. Chill for 3 hours. Once the mixture is ready, churn it in an ice cream machine for about 20 minutes and serve immediately as soft serve or freeze for 4 hours if you prefer a firmer texture.

Lemon-Glazed Persimmon Bars

Sometimes you need a bar instead of a cookie or a cake or even a pudding. In this particular bar, the glaze has a perfect tartness that offsets the sweet persimmon-y flavor of the bar. Yum!

BARS

INGREDIENTS

1 cup persimmon pulp

1½ teaspoon baking soda

1 ¾ cups flour

1 teaspoon salt

1 teaspoon cinnamon

1 teaspoon nutmeg

1 egg, beaten

1 cup sugar

½ cup salad oil

1 cup raisins

1 cup chopped walnuts (optional)

1½ teaspoons lemon juice

ICING GLAZE

1 cup powdered sugar

2 tablespoons lemon juice

3 to 4 tablespoons of milk (as needed)

DIRECTIONS

Mix the persimmon pulp, baking soda and lemon juice; set aside. In a separate bowl, combine the flour, salt, cinnamon and nutmeg. In a third bowl, stir together the egg, sugar, oil, and raisins. Alternate adding the flour mixture and the persimmon mixture into the raisin mixture, stirring until just blended. Stir in the nuts. Put into a greased and floured 10-by-15-inch jelly roll pan. Bake at 350 degrees for 20 to 25 minutes until springy. Meanwhile, mix the powdered sugar and lemon juice for the icing glaze in a small bowl. Stir until smooth. Add 3 to 4 tablespoons of milk if the consistency is too thick to drizzle. Set aside. Let the bars cool for just a few minutes before spreading the icing glaze over the top. Cut into bars.

The Perfect Persimmon Pancakes

INGREDIENTS

1 cup white whole wheat flour

1 teaspoon baking powder

1 teaspoon cinnamon

¼ teaspoon nutmeg

½ cup ripe persimmon pulp

1 egg

1 tablespoon melted butter

1 teaspoon vanilla extract

1 cup milk (¾ cup for thicker batter)

DIRECTIONS

Mix together the flour, baking powder, cinnamon, and nutmeg. Puree the ripe persimmon pulp until smooth. Next stir the egg, butter, vanilla extract, and persimmon puree into the dry ingredients. Slowly whisk in the milk until well combined. Heat a skillet to medium heat and pour a ¼-cup scoop of batter. Cook for 1 to 2 minutes on each side. Repeat until batter is finished. Serve immediately. Top with butter, syrup, or even coconut flakes, or simply sprinkle a bit of powdered sugar on top.

Fresh, hot cinnamon rolls covered with cream cheese icing.
Photo by author.

Cinnamon Rolls with a Persimmon Kick

Who doesn't love the smell of cinnamon rolls baking in the morning? Or how about some pancakes drizzled in warm syrup to start your day? If you're a "give me carbs for breakfast" kind of person, then you'll love these next two recipes.

DOUGH

1 cup milk

2 teaspoons instant dry yeast

2 eggs

1 teaspoon salt

⅓ cup butter, melted

½ cup sugar

4½ cups flour

FILLING

½ cup butter, softened

1 cup packed brown sugar

2 tablespoons cinnamon

¼ cup heavy cream

¼ cup persimmon pulp

CREAM CHEESE ICING

½ cup butter, softened

8 ounces cream cheese

2 teaspoons vanilla extract

3 cups powdered sugar

DIRECTIONS

Preheat the oven to 375 degrees. Grease a large baking sheet.

In a large bowl, combine the milk, yeast, eggs, salt, butter, and sugar. Mix in the flour using a mixer, then put the mixture to the side for 5 minutes or so. Spray a large bowl with cooking spray, add the dough, and set the bowl to the side so the dough can rise, about 40 minutes.

For the filling, in a medium-size bowl, mix together the butter, brown sugar, and cinnamon.

Next, sprinkle a pastry mat (approximately 23-by-15 inches) with flour. Using a rolling pin, roll the dough across the mat. Smooth the cinnamon filling over the entirety of the dough. Working from the long end, roll up the dough. Cut into 12 slices and place them onto the greased baking sheet. Cover the sheet for 15 to 20 minutes and let the rolls rise.

Warm the heavy cream and persimmon pulp in a small pan and pour over the rolls. Let it soak down into the rolls. Bake until the rolls are cooked through and golden-colored on top—usually 15 to 20 minutes.

For the cream cheese icing, beat together the butter and cream cheese. Add the vanilla extract. Next, add the powdered sugar one cup at a time and beat on low speed until smooth. Spread over the cooled rolls.

Persimmon Muffins

Yes, I admit it—I love carbs. I know that's not a very vogue statement to make in this age of keto-diet frenzy, but I do. I've always believed we can enjoy all food groups in moderation (unless your doctor has said otherwise), so have a persimmon muffin or a piece of persimmon bread. I promise, they are worth every carb.

INGREDIENTS

2 cups flour

1 teaspoon baking soda

1 teaspoon baking powder

¼ teaspoon salt

1 teaspoon cinnamon

1 cup persimmon pulp

¼ cup vegetable oil

2 eggs

½ cup organic honey

½ cup raisins (optional)

½ cup walnuts (optional)

DIRECTIONS

Preheat the oven to 350 degrees. In a large bowl, combine all the flour, baking soda, baking powder, salt, and cinnamon. Next, combine the persimmon pulp, oil, eggs, and honey in a blender or a food processor, or simply use a mixer and mix well. Add this mixture to the dry ingredients. Stir until the flour mixture is moist and free from lumps. Stir in any optional ingredients. Line your muffin tin with paper liners or spray with a nonstick spray. Spoon mixture into each muffin opening. Bake at 350 degrees for 15 to 20 minutes or until "the toothpick test" reveals a clean toothpick after inserting it into the middle of the muffin. Make sure not to overcook.

Persimmon Bread

How about some warm persimmon bread with some persimmon-orange marmalade to top it off? If that sounds yummy to you, you're in luck.

INGREDIENTS

1 cup raisins

3½ cups flour

2 teaspoons baking soda

1 teaspoon cinnamon

½ teaspoon nutmeg

1 teaspoon salt

1 cup chopped nuts (optional)

3 cups sugar

1 cup oil

2 cups pulp

⅔ cup water, plus 1 cup hot water for soaking raisins

DIRECTIONS

Cover the raisins in 1 cup hot water and leave to soak for 2 to 3 minutes. Preheat the oven to 325 degrees. Grease a 9-by-5-by-3-inch loaf pan and set aside.

In a medium-size bowl, mix the flour, baking soda, cinnamon, nutmeg, salt, and nuts. Drain the raisins and add them to the flour mixture. In another bowl, blend the eggs, sugar, water, and oil. Next, add the pulp to the sugar mixture. Fold in the flour mixture, and then pour the batter into the prepared pan. Bake for 50 minutes or until an inserted toothpick comes out clean.

Persimmon & Orange Marmalade

INGREDIENTS

7 large ripe persimmons, peeled

1¼ cup sugar

1 orange, juiced

2½ tablespoons water

1½ tablespoons cornstarch

DIRECTIONS

Place the persimmons in a food processor and pulse until pureed. Place the puree into a saucepan over medium-high heat and add the sugar. Boil for 10 to 15 minutes, stirring occasionally. In a separate bowl, mix the orange juice, water, and cornstarch, then add this mixture to the saucepan. Heat for 15 minutes, stirring often. Once thickened, remove from the heat and cool to room temperature. Finally, place the mixture into jars, seal them, and place the jars into the fridge or freezer. (If placed in the fridge, consume the contents within the next seven days.)

Persimmon Date Loaf

INGREDIENTS

1½ cups flour

2 teaspoons baking soda

2 teaspoons baking powder

½ teaspoon salt

1 cup sugar

½ cup graham cracker crumbs

1 cup persimmon pulp

1 cup chopped dates

1 cup chopped nuts (optional)

½ teaspoon vanilla

2 tablespoons softened butter

½ cup half-and-half

DIRECTIONS

Sift together the flour, baking soda, baking powder, and salt. Next, add the remaining ingredients and mix well. Grease a 9-by-5-by-3-inch loaf pan and pour the batter into it. Bake at 350 degrees for about 1 hour or until the loaf pulls away from the sides of the pan.

Persimmon Fudge

I've always had a difficult time making fudge—even those no-fail recipes. But this particular recipe has never failed me. Just be careful not to overcook, and you'll also have success.

INGREDIENTS

1 cup persimmon pulp

¾ cup butter

⅔ cup evaporated milk

3 cups sugar

2 cups marshmallow cream

1 teaspoon maple syrup

2 cups powdered sugar

DIRECTIONS

Combine the persimmon pulp, butter, milk and sugar in a saucepan over high heat. Bring the ingredients to a boil, stirring constantly until the mixture reaches the soft-ball stage (syrup dropped into cold water will form a soft ball). Quickly remove from the heat. Next, add the marshmallow cream, maple syrup, and powdered sugar. Mix well. Pour the mixture into a greased 9-by-13-inch pan. Let it cool before cutting into even squares.

Persimmon Spice Muffins

INGREDIENTS

3 cups flour

2 teaspoons cinnamon

¼ teaspoon cloves

½ teaspoon ginger

¼ teaspoon nutmeg

1 teaspoon baking soda

½ teaspoon salt

1⅓ cups vegetable oil

3 eggs

1 teaspoon vanilla extract

6 firm Fuyu persimmons, peeled
and chopped finely

½ cup wheat germ

2 cups sugar

DIRECTIONS

Preheat the oven to 350 degrees. Prepare two twelve-cup muffin tins with cooking spray or muffin liners.

Sift the flour, cinnamon, cloves, ginger, nutmeg, baking soda, and salt into a bowl. Put the oil, eggs, and vanilla into a bowl and beat with a stand mixer until the mixture is yellow and light. (This will take 4 to 5 minutes.) Turn the mixer on low and gradually add the dry ingredients. Then add the finely chopped persimmons, wheat germ, and sugar and stir.

Divide the batter evenly among the muffin tins. Bake for 25 minutes or until a tester comes out clean. Remove and cool on a rack.

White Chocolate Mousse Persimmon Gingerbread Trifle

Submitted by a fellow writer friend of mine, Jennifer Watts, this persimmon concoction is a bit more complicated than most of the recipes in this book, but it's so good, I had to include it. If you're a chocoholic but you also love persimmons, you'll adore it. Jennifer combined three different recipes to create this one.

WHITE CHOCOLATE MOUSSE

- ½ cup whipping cream
- ½ cup chopped white chocolate or white chocolate chips
- 4 ounces cream cheese
- 1 to 3 tablespoons powdered sugar, divided
- ½ teaspoon vanilla extract
- ½ teaspoon salt

CHUNKY PERSIMMON PUREE

- 6 to 8 Fuyu persimmons

GINGERBREAD

- 1½ cups all-purpose flour, spooned into a measuring cup and leveled off with the back edge of knife

- 1 teaspoon baking soda
- ½ teaspoon salt
- 2 teaspoons ground ginger
- 1 teaspoon ground cinnamon
- ¼ teaspoon ground cloves
- 4 tablespoons unsalted butter, cut into ½-inch chunks
- ⅔ cup dark brown sugar
- ⅔ cup mild-flavor molasses, such as Grandma's Original (not robust or blackstrap)
- ⅔ cup boiling water
- 1 large egg

DIRECTIONS

For the mousse, in a medium mixing bowl, beat the whipping cream at high speed until stiff peaks form. Set the bowl aside. Gently melt the white chocolate in a small pot over low heat or in the microwave at half power in 30-second increments, stirring frequently. Using the same beaters you used to beat the whipping cream, beat the cream cheese and one tablespoon of powdered sugar until light and fluffy. Beat in the white chocolate, vanilla extract, and salt on medium speed until well combined. Fold in the whipped cream. If it's not combining easily, use the mixer to beat it in on the very lowest setting, just until combined. Do not over beat!

Taste the mousse, and if it's not sweet enough, fold in a tablespoon or two of powdered sugar until the mousse is sweet enough for your liking. Serve immediately or refrigerate for 1 to 2 hours for a firmer version. Refrigerate any leftovers for up to two days.

For the chunky persimmon puree, peel the skin off the persimmons and cut into cubes. Place the cut persimmons into a food processor and pulse until slightly pureed but a little chunky.

For the gingerbread, preheat the oven to 350 degrees. Grease a 9-by-9-inch square pan with nonstick cooking spray. Add a few tablespoons of flour to the pan; shake and turn until the bottom and sides are evenly coated with a light dusting of flour. Holding the pan upside down over the sink, tap out any excess flour.

In a medium bowl, whisk together the flour, baking soda, salt, ginger, cinnamon, and cloves. Set aside. In a large bowl, combine the butter, dark brown sugar, molasses, and boiling water. Whisk until the butter is melted. When the mixture is lukewarm, whisk in the egg.

Add the dry ingredients to the wet ingredients and whisk until just combined with no more lumps. Pour the batter into the prepared pan and bake for about 35 minutes or until the edges look dark and the middle feels firm to the touch. Set the pan on a rack to cool slightly, then cut into ¼- to ½-inch squares. Layer half the small gingerbread cubes at the bottom of a decorative glass dish. Add half of the chunky persimmon purée over the gingerbread. Then spread half the white chocolate mousse over the persimmon layer. Repeat with the remaining gingerbread, purée, and mousse. Garnish with mint sprigs, ground cinnamon, nutmeg, and white chocolate shavings. Yields 6 to 8 servings.

Persimmon Jam

INGREDIENTS

2½ cups Fuyu persimmon puree
   (3 to 4 large persimmons)

1 cup water

¼ teaspoon salt

3 tablespoons lemon juice

3 tablespoons pectin

½ tablespoons unsalted butter

1 cup sugar

4 to 5 half-pint jars

DIRECTIONS

Put the puree, water, salt, lemon juice, pectin, and butter in the bottom of a large pot. Bring the mixture to a simmer and cook for 5 minutes. Add the sugar and stir. Bring the mixture to a boil and boil hard for 1 minute. Then turn off the heat. Pour the jam into sterilized jars while hot.

Zesty Persimmon Jam

INGREDIENTS

4 cups ripe persimmon pulp

3 cups sugar

2 tablespoons lemon juice

1 teaspoon lime juice

½ teaspoon lemon zest

DIRECTIONS

Puree the ripe persimmon pulp until smooth. Combine the persimmon puree and sugar in a large pan and cook over low heat. Stir 3 minutes or until thickened. Make sure you don't let it come to a boil. Next, remove from the heat and stir in the lemon juice, lime juice, and zest. Pour the mixture into jars and store in the fridge for a couple of months or store in a freezer for up to a year.

Cinnamon Persimmon Cookies

INGREDIENTS

½ cup softened butter

1 cup brown sugar

1 egg

1 cup persimmon pulp

2 cups flour

1 teaspoon baking soda

2 teaspoons cinnamon

¼ teaspoon salt

1 teaspoon vanilla

DIRECTIONS

Preheat the oven to 350 degrees. Cream the butter and sugar together. Add the egg and persimmon pulp and mix. Sift together the flour, baking soda, cinnamon, and salt and add to the persimmon mixture. Stir in the vanilla. Drop large spoonfuls onto a cookie sheet, keeping in mind that the cookies will not spread in the oven. Bake for 12 minutes or until the cookies are lightly brown around the edges.

Walnut Persimmon Cookies

INGREDIENTS

2 cups flour

½ teaspoon baking soda

½ teaspoon baking powder

½ teaspoon cinnamon

½ teaspoon ground cloves

½ teaspoon ground nutmeg

½ teaspoon salt

½ cup shortening

1 cup white sugar

½ teaspoon vanilla

1 egg

1 cup persimmon pulp (about 2 large very ripe persimmons)

½ cup chopped crystallized ginger

½ cup chopped walnuts

DIRECTIONS

Preheat the oven to 350 degrees. Sift together the flour, baking soda, baking powder, cinnamon, cloves, nutmeg, and salt. Beat the shortening and sugar with a mixer for about 5 minutes. Add in the vanilla, egg, and persimmon pulp. Mix well. With the mixer on low, gradually beat in the flour mixture. Fold in the ginger and walnuts. Drop by teaspoonfuls about 2 inches apart onto cookie sheets, keeping in mind that these cookies will not spread while baking. Bake for 12 to 15 minutes or until the cookies' edges are firm. Let the cookies cool on the sheets for 1 minute before moving to wire racks to finish cooling.

Pleasant Persimmon Cupcakes

INGREDIENTS

1½ cups flour

1 teaspoon pumpkin pie spice

1 teaspoon baking soda

½ cup butter, room temperature

1½ cups sugar

2 large eggs

¾ cup persimmon pulp

½ cup orange juice

FROSTING

¾ cup sugar

½ teaspoon ground ginger

2 large eggs

1½ cups persimmon pulp

12 ounces evaporated milk

DIRECTIONS

For the cupcakes, preheat the oven to 350 degrees and prepare a muffin tin with paper cupcake liners. In a medium bowl, whisk together the flour, pumpkin pie spice, and baking soda. In a separate bowl, cream the butter and sugar. Mix in the eggs, persimmon pulp, and orange juice until combined. Slowly add the flour mixture and mix until combined. Fill the cupcake liners ¾ full with batter. Bake for 30 minutes or until a toothpick can be inserted and removed clean.

For the frosting, place all ingredients in a saucepan and cook over medium heat. Stir continuously until the mixture comes to a boil. Allow to boil for about 1 minute, then remove it from the heat and let it cool to room temperature. Refrigerate for 3 hours, then pipe the frosting onto cooled cupcakes.

Orange-Glazed Persimmon Cookies

INGREDIENTS

1 cup ripe persimmon pulp

½ cup butter (room temperature)

½ cup white sugar

½ cup brown sugar

1 egg

1 teaspoon vanilla

½ teaspoon baking soda

1 teaspoon orange zest

2 cups flour

2 teaspoons baking powder

1 teaspoon cinnamon

½ teaspoon salt

1 cup walnuts, dried cranberries, raisins, and/or dates

GLAZE

2 cups powdered sugar

2 teaspoons orange juice

1 teaspoon grated orange peel

DIRECTIONS

For the cookies, puree the ripe persimmon pulp until smooth. Reserve one tablespoon puree for the frosting. In a large bowl, beat together the butter and sugars. Then beat in the egg and vanilla. Finally, mix in the persimmon puree, baking soda, and orange zest. In a separate bowl, whisk together the flour, baking powder, cinnamon, and salt. Slowly add the dry ingredients to the persimmon mixture. Then stir in the nuts and/or dried fruit. Chill the dough for one hour.

Preheat the oven to 350 degrees. Drop the cookie dough in 1-inch rounds onto nonstick cookie sheets, leaving at least an inch between the cookies. Bake for 13 to 14 minutes or until the cookies are lightly browned around the edges. Let cool on a wire rack before frosting.

For the frosting, sift the powdered sugar and whisk it with the orange juice until smooth. Add the reserved tablespoon of persimmon puree and the orange zest, and mix until smooth. Dip a spoon into the glaze and drizzle it over the cookies; let the glaze harden before serving.

Ginger Persimmon Scones

INGREDIENTS

2 cups flour

⅓ cup sugar

2 teaspoons baking powder

½ teaspoon baking soda

¼ teaspoon salt

¼ teaspoon ground ginger

½ cup butter, cut into cubes

1 cup buttermilk

2 Fuyu persimmons, peeled and diced

¼ cup candied ginger, chopped

1 egg, whisked with 1 tablespoon milk

DIRECTIONS

Preheat the oven to 350 degrees. Prepare a 12-cup muffin tin with cooking spray or butter.

In a large bowl, whisk together the flour, sugar, baking powder, baking soda, salt, and ground ginger. Add the butter cubes and mix until the butter is broken into pea-size chunks. Make a well in the middle of the mixture to add the buttermilk, then stir until it's almost incorporated. Add the chopped persimmons and candied ginger and fold until they're evenly distributed.

Divide the dough among the muffin cups and lightly brush the tops with the beaten egg. Bake for 20 to 25 minutes or until the tops are evenly golden brown. An inserted toothpick should come out clean. Let cool until the scones are firm enough to remove from the tins, and serve warm.

Apple Cinnamon Persimmon Muffins

INGREDIENTS

1½ cups flour

½ cup oats

⅓ cup brown sugar

3 teaspoons baking powder

2 teaspoons ground cinnamon

½ teaspoon salt

2 persimmons, peeled and finely chopped

1 apple, peeled, cored, and finely chopped

2 tablespoons butter, melted

1 egg

½ cup water

TOPPING

¼ cup brown sugar

½ tablespoon ground cinnamon

DIRECTIONS

Preheat the oven to 375 degrees. Grease a muffin tin or insert paper muffin liners.

Combine the flour, oats, sugar, baking powder, cinnamon, and salt. Add the chopped persimmons, chopped apple, butter, and egg to the flour mixture. Mix to coat the fruit, then add the water. Stir until combined. Fill each muffin cup about ⅔ full.

For the topping, mix the brown sugar and cinnamon together and sprinkle it on top of the muffins. Bake for 20 minutes and let cool for 5 minutes in the muffin tin.

Proper Persimmon Pound Cake

INGREDIENTS

2½ cups flour

¾ cup sugar

½ teaspoon baking powder

2 teaspoons baking soda

½ teaspoon salt

2 eggs

2 cups persimmon pulp

1 cup milk

2 teaspoons vanilla

DIRECTIONS

Preheat the oven to 300 degrees. Grease and flour a 9-by-13-inch loaf or Bundt pan.

Whisk together the flour, sugar, baking powder, baking soda, and salt. Set aside. In a separate bowl, whisk together the eggs, persimmon pulp, milk, and vanilla until smooth. Fold the wet mixture into the dry mixture until no lumps remain. Pour the batter into the prepared pan.

Bake for 1 hour and 45 minutes or until a toothpick inserted into the center comes out clean. Cool in the pan for 10 minutes, then transfer the cake from the pan to a wire rack to cool completely. Top with icing if desired.

Peppy Persimmon Pumpkin Bars

INGREDIENTS

4 eggs

1 cup sugar

½ cup brown sugar

¾ cup vegetable oil

4 ounces applesauce

¾ cup very ripe Hachiya persimmon pulp

1¼ cup canned pumpkin

1½ teaspoons baking powder

1½ teaspoons baking soda

1 teaspoon salt

1 teaspoon cinnamon

½ teaspoon cloves

½ teaspoon ginger

½ teaspoon pumpkin spice

2 cups flour

CREAM CHEESE FROSTING

8 ounces cream cheese, softened

2 tablespoons butter, softened

2 cups powdered sugar

1 teaspoon vanilla extract

DIRECTIONS

For the pumpkin bars, preheat the oven to 350 degrees. Combine the eggs, sugar, brown sugar, oil, applesauce, persimmon pulp, and pumpkin and mix until creamy. Mix in all the dry ingredients, saving the flour for last. Pour the batter into a greased 9-by-13-inch pan and bake for 45 minutes, until the batter is firm to the touch.

For the cream cheese frosting, in a separate bowl, mix the cream cheese and butter until smooth. Gradually mix in the powdered sugar and vanilla. Wait until the cake has cooled and spread the icing on it.

Maple-Persimmon Upside-Down Cake

INGREDIENTS

8 tablespoons butter, separated

1 cup and 2 tablespoons real maple syrup

1½ cups flour

1 teaspoon baking powder

½ teaspoon baking soda

½ teaspoon salt

½ teaspoon ground cinnamon

¼ teaspoon ground nutmeg

1 large egg, room temperature

1 large egg yolk, room temperature

⅔ cup buttermilk

½ cup roasted pecans, finely chopped

2 ripe Fuyu persimmons

MAPLE CREAM

1 cup heavy whipping cream, chilled

2 tablespoons real maple syrup, chilled

⅛ teaspoon ground cinnamon

DIRECTIONS

Preheat the oven to 350 degrees.

In a skillet, melt 2 tablespoons of butter and 2 tablespoons of maple syrup on low heat for about 1 minute or until completely melted. Remove from the heat.

In a large bowl, whisk together the flour, baking powder, baking soda, salt, cinnamon, and nutmeg. Set aside.

Beat the remaining 6 tablespoons of butter and 1 cup maple syrup with a stand mixer for about 2 minutes on medium-low. Add in the egg and egg yolk and beat for another minute. Add half of the flour mixture and beat for 10 seconds. Add the buttermilk and beat for 10 more seconds. Add the rest of the flour mixture and beat for 30 seconds. Scrape down the bowl and stir in the pecans.

Pour the melted butter and maple mixture into a 10-inch cake pan, making sure to cover the bottom. Cut the persimmons into horizontal slices, about ¼ inch thick, and place them on top of the butter and maple mixture. Set one slice in the middle, then layer the slices in circles around the center slice until the bottom of the pan is completely covered. Pour the batter over the persimmon slices and smooth the surface.

Bake on the center rack for 45 to 50 minutes, rotating the pan about 20 minutes into baking. The cake will brown slightly and will be done when an inserted toothpick comes out clean.

Remove the pan from the oven and allow to cool until it can be touched without oven mitts. Using a butter knife, loosen the sides of the cake. Place a large serving plate upside down on top of the pan. Holding the plate on the pan, flip the cake over, out of the pan, and onto the plate.

To make the maple cream, whip the cream, maple syrup, and cinnamon together. Serve slices of the cake warm with a dollop of the maple cream.

HEALTHY PERSIMMON RECIPES

While I love a good dessert, and persimmon pudding is my all-time favorite, I also balance that sweet tooth of mine with healthy dishes and a daily dose of cardio. One such healthy option is a persimmon smoothie. All the yumminess, none of the guilt. Enjoy!

Practically Guilt-Free Persimmon Smoothie

INGREDIENTS

1 frozen banana

1 Fuyu persimmon

¼ teaspoon ground cinnamon

½ teaspoon vanilla essence or vanilla extract or ¼ teaspoon almond extract

1 cup unsweetened almond milk or coconut milk

3 ice cubes

Stevia to taste

Low-fat whipped topping (optional)

DIRECTIONS

Put all ingredients, except the whipped topping, into a blender and mix on high until smooth. Pour into a tall glass and top with a bit of low-fat whipped topping. (The variety I use has only 15 calories per 2 tablespoons.) Drink up!

Low-Carb Persimmon Pudding

Okay, so maybe you've been trying to drop a few pounds. Or maybe you are watching your carb intake. Well, I've got you covered by way of Ken Row, who adapted this recipe from a favorite served at Spring Mill Inn in southern Indiana. While it might not be "keto approved," it's certainly a better alternative for you carb counters than most every other dessert recipe in this book. Thanks, Ken. Our hips are appreciative.

INGREDIENTS

¾ cup buttermilk

¾ cup heavy cream

1 teaspoon baking soda

1 teaspoon baking powder

2 cups persimmon pulp

1½ cups Swerve confectioners' sugar

24 short squirts liquid Splenda

3 eggs, beaten

⅛ teaspoon salt

1 teaspoon vanilla

½ teaspoon cinnamon

1¼ cups almond flour

2 tablespoons coconut flour

½ stick butter

DIRECTIONS

Preheat the oven to 325 degrees. Mix the buttermilk, cream, baking soda, and baking powder together; set aside and let foam. Mix the pulp, Swerve confectioners' sugar, Splenda, eggs, salt, vanilla, and cinnamon together. Add to the buttermilk mixture and then gradually add the flours. Mix well. Melt the butter in a 9-by-13-inch pan, and coat the pan with it. Pour the batter into the pan and bake for 45 minutes or until an inserted toothpick comes out clean. The edges of the pudding should begin pulling away from the sides of the pan and the center should appear golden.

Persimmon Carrot Cake

So, I realize a "healthy dessert" sounds like an oxymoron, but this persimmon carrot cake might come close. Carrots have biotin, vitamin K, vitamin B6, and more! And both carrots and persimmons contain vitamin A. This persimmon carrot cake is a win-win—it tastes amazing, and it's semi-good for you. So, go ahead and indulge a little!

INGREDIENTS

2 cups flour

2 teaspoons baking soda

2 teaspoons baking powder

1 teaspoon salt

2 teaspoons cinnamon

2 medium eggs

1½ cups oil

1½ cups granulated sugar

1 cup persimmon pulp

1 tablespoon orange zest

1 teaspoon vanilla extract

3 cups shredded carrots

¼ cup chopped nuts

½ cup raisins (optional)

CREAM CHEESE ICING

½ cup softened butter

8 ounces cream cheese

2 teaspoons vanilla extract

3 cups powdered sugar

DIRECTIONS

For the cake, preheat the oven to 350 degrees. Grease a 10-inch Bundt pan; sprinkle with flour, and set aside for later. Sift together the flour, baking soda, baking powder, salt, and cinnamon in a bowl and set aside. Next, in a large mixing bowl, beat together the eggs and oil before adding the sugar, persimmon pulp, orange zest, and vanilla extract. To finish up, add the dry mixture, the carrots, the nuts, and the raisins. Carefully pour the batter into the pan and bake for approximately 50 minutes, until an inserted toothpick comes out clean. Let the cake cool. Tap the sides of the Bundt pan a few times with a spatula before flipping it over and placing the cake onto a serving plate.

For the cream cheese icing, beat together the butter and cream cheese with a mixer, then add the vanilla extract. Next, add the powdered sugar one cup at a time and beat on low speed until smooth. Ice the cooled cake with the cream cheese icing or simply dust some powdered sugar on top and enjoy.

PERSIMMONS ARE GOOD FOR MORE THAN JUST DESSERTS

I've never been much of a hummus fan, but having lived in Texas for a decade, I like a little kick to my food. This hot persimmon hummus has just enough heat and the right amount of sweet to be interesting. Pair it with crackers or enjoy atop some fresh vegetables.

Hot Persimmon Hummus

INGREDIENTS

¼ cup tahini

1 (16-ounce) can garbanzo beans, drained

1 tablespoon minced fresh ginger

1 teaspoon pink Himalayan salt

¼ cup orange juice

¼ cup persimmon pulp

1 tablespoon lime juice

DIRECTIONS

Mix all ingredients in a blender until smooth and serve with veggies or crackers. Yields 1½ cups.

Healthy Persimmon Nut Bread

With just a few substitutions, even a fattening recipe can be somewhat healthy. As you'll notice, in this recipe I replaced regular flour with whole wheat flour, canola oil with coconut oil, and whole milk with nonfat milk. Try it—I doubt you'll even notice these healthy replacements. Remember, little changes can eventually produce big results.

INGREDIENTS

1 cup ripe persimmon pulp	1½ all-purpose flour
2 eggs, beaten	½ cup wheat germ
½ cup coconut oil	3 teaspoons cinnamon
½ cup sugar	2 teaspoons baking soda
½ cup brown sugar	1 teaspoon baking powder
½ cup nonfat milk	1 teaspoon salt
½ cup water	1 cup raisins
2 cups whole wheat flour	½ cup chopped walnuts

DIRECTIONS

Preheat the oven to 350 degrees. Puree the ripe persimmon pulp until smooth. Combine the persimmon puree, beaten eggs, oil, sugar, brown sugar, milk, and water in a large bowl, and mix well. In another bowl sift together the flours. Combine the sifted flours with the wheat germ, cinnamon, baking soda, baking powder, and salt, and then add the mixture to the persimmon batter. Beat well. Stir in the raisins and nuts. Pour the batter into two loaf pans and bake for 45 to 50 minutes or until an inserted toothpick comes out clean.

Persimmon Vegetable Soup

Is there anything more comforting on a cold day than a big bowl of piping hot vegetable soup? If you're a fan of vegetable soup, you'll love this interpretation of it. With the persimmon puree and the added pasta, this soup feels hearty. When I fix it at home, my husband insists on corn muffins as well. I have to say, they make a deliciously satisfying pairing on a cold winter day in Indiana.

INGREDIENTS

½ cup ripe persimmon pulp

2 onions, diced

1 red bell pepper, chopped

½ cup chopped celery

½ cup chopped carrots

2 teaspoons minced garlic

2 tablespoons olive oil

2 (15-ounce) cans white lima beans

1 quart chicken broth, divided

1 (8-ounce) can tomato sauce

2 tablespoons fresh rosemary

¼ teaspoon salt

½ cup whole grain pasta

DIRECTIONS

Puree the ripe persimmon pulp until smooth. Sauté the onions, red bell pepper, celery, carrots, garlic, and oil in a large soup pot for 5 minutes. Drain the beans and puree half of them in a food processor with ½ cup chicken broth and the tomato sauce. Add the rest of the broth, the rosemary, the persimmon puree, the bean puree, and the remaining beans to the vegetables and bring to a boil over medium heat. Simmer and cover for 40 minutes. Serves 6 to 8.

Skinny Persimmon Whip

This is a quick and easy snack, breakfast, or dessert. I like to add a few coconut flakes on top of this whip, or try a favorite topping of your own!

INGREDIENTS

2 tablespoons ripe persimmon pulp

⅓ cup dry nonfat milk

⅓ cup nonfat sour cream

¾ teaspoon cinnamon

2 teaspoon stevia

DIRECTIONS

Puree the ripe persimmon pulp until smooth. Using a handheld mixer, beat together the dry nonfat milk and the sour cream for one to two minutes on high. Add the cinnamon and stevia and continue to beat for another 2 minutes. Last, stir in the persimmon puree. Serve immediately.

Scrumptious Persimmon Salad

I've always been a big fan of salad, and this persimmon salad is one of my favorites. I especially like the dressing, but I don't put it all over the salad. Instead, I put it in a side dish and simply dip my salad bites into it. Not only will that little tip save you a few calories, but it will keep you from drowning the flavorful salad with a strong balsamic dressing.

SALAD

8 dried persimmons, chopped and seeded

1½ tablespoon brown sugar

½ tablespoon oregano

1½ tablespoon balsamic vinegar

½ cup red wine

¾ cup candied walnuts

8 cups mixed salad greens

½ cup reduced-fat feta cheese

BALSAMIC VINAIGRETTE

3 tablespoons balsamic vinegar

1½ teaspoons Dijon mustard

½ cup olive oil

½ teaspoon salt

½ teaspoon crushed black pepper

DIRECTIONS

For the salad, combine the persimmons, brown sugar, oregano, balsamic vinegar, and red wine in a glass 9-by-13 baking dish. Bake for 30 minutes, stirring halfway through. Cool.

For the vinaigrette, whisk all the ingredients together.

Combine the cooled toasted persimmons, candied walnuts, mixed salad greens, and feta in a large bowl and toss together with the dressing. Serves 6 to 8.

Persimmon Spinach Salad

INGREDIENTS

4 to 5 ounces baby spinach

1 large Fuyu persimmon, cut in ½-inch chunks

⅓ cup dried cranberries

⅓ cup feta cheese

⅓ cup toasted pecan pieces

VINAIGRETTE

2 tablespoons orange juice

1½ tablespoons apple cider vinegar

1 tablespoon maple syrup

1½ teaspoons Dijon mustard

1 teaspoon lemon juice

¼ cup extra virgin olive oil

salt and pepper to taste

DIRECTIONS

For the salad, toss the spinach, persimmon chunks, dried cranberries, feta, and pecans in a large bowl.

For the vinaigrette, put the orange juice, vinegar, maple syrup, mustard, lemon juice, olive oil, salt, and pepper together in a small jar. Close the lid and shake to combine. Pour the dressing over the salad and serve immediately.

Fuyu Persimmon Salad

One of my dear California friends swears by this next salad. She promises to make it for me the next time I visit her. I can't wait!

DRESSING

¼ cup persimmon pulp

2 tablespoon lemon juice

3 teaspoon water

1½ tablespoons tahini

¼ cup olive oil

¼ teaspoon pink Himalayan salt

¼ teaspoon black pepper

SALAD

3 ripe Fuyu persimmons, peeled, seeded, and sliced

3 ripe avocados, pitted and sliced

8 cups spinach

DIRECTIONS

For the dressing, puree the persimmon pulp until smooth. Blend together the puree, lemon juice, water, and tahini until a creamy consistency is reached. Slowly add the oil, salt, and pepper.

Gently mix together the persimmons, avocados, spinach, and dressing. Makes 4 to 6 servings.

Persimmon Applesauce

INGREDIENTS

6 medium apples

4 Fuyu persimmons

Juice of one lemon

2 teaspoons vanilla

½ cup water

DIRECTIONS

Peel, core, and thinly slice the apples and persimmons. Place them in a slow cooker and add the lemon juice, vanilla, and water. Cover the slow cooker and set the temperature to high. Let the mixture cook until the fruit is softened (3 to 6 hours, depending on the strength of the slow cooker).

Once the fruit is softened, mash it with a potato masher until you've achieved your desired consistency. Store in an airtight container in the fridge until you are ready to serve.

Shakshuka with Persimmons

INGREDIENTS

1 tablespoon extra virgin olive oil

1 large yellow onion, thinly sliced

2 red bell peppers, seeded and sliced

2 garlic cloves, minced

1 pound persimmons, coarsely chopped

1 tablespoon tomato paste

2 teaspoons paprika

1 teaspoon Aleppo pepper

¼ teaspoon coriander

½ teaspoon cumin

4 cups canned chopped tomatoes

Salt and pepper to taste

5 eggs

DIRECTIONS

Preheat the oven to 375 degrees. Heat the olive oil in a large Dutch oven over medium heat. Add the onion and sauté until softened and transparent, about 10 minutes, stirring every 2 to 3 minutes. Add the bell peppers and cook for 8 to 10 minutes, stirring every couple of minutes, until the peppers have softened. Add the garlic and stir for 3 to 5 minutes. Add the persimmons, tomato paste, paprika, Aleppo pepper, coriander, and cumin. Cook until the persimmons have softened, 6 to 8 minutes. Add the chopped tomatoes and bring the mixture to a boil. Reduce the heat to medium low and continue cooking for 10 minutes.

Turn off the heat and add the salt and pepper to taste. Use the back of a spoon to create 5 wells in the top of the shakshuka and crack an egg into each one. Place the Dutch oven in the oven and bake until the egg whites are barely set and the yolks are still jiggly, 7 to 10 minutes. Watch carefully for the last few minutes to make sure you don't overcook the eggs. Remove from the oven and serve.

Persimmon-y Easy Overnight Oats

INGREDIENTS

½ cup peeled and diced persimmon

1 tablespoon shredded coconut

½ cup rolled oats

½ cup milk

1½ tablespoons honey

DIRECTIONS

Mix together all ingredients and store in a glass jar. Refrigerate covered overnight for about 8 to 10 hours until you are ready to serve.

Persimmon Orange Smoothie

INGREDIENTS

1 ripe persimmon

1 cup orange juice

¼ banana

¼ teaspoon vanilla

Ice (if desired)

DIRECTIONS

Peel the persimmon and cut it into large cubes. Place all ingredients in a blender and blend until smooth. Transfer the smoothie to a glass and serve immediately.

Persimmon Pomegranate Fruit Salad

INGREDIENTS

3 Fuyu persimmons

1 Granny Smith apple

¾ cup pomegranate seeds

2 teaspoons lemon juice

1 teaspoon honey

DIRECTIONS

Peel and chop the persimmons and apple. Gently toss all ingredients until well mixed. Serve within 3 days.

Cranberry Persimmon Harvest Salad

INGREDIENTS

½ cup walnuts

½ cup pepitas

2 tablespoons maple syrup

Sea salt

3 cups baby kale or arugula

3 Fuyu persimmons, cored and cut into wedges

2 clementines, peeled and chopped

¾ cups dried cranberries

8 ounces burrata cheese

BALSAMIC DRESSING

¼ cup cranberry juice

¼ cup balsamic vinegar

1 tablespoon lemon juice

⅓ cup olive oil

Salt and pepper to taste

DIRECTIONS

For the salad, combine the walnuts, pepitas, and maple syrup in a medium skillet and place over medium heat for 5 minutes, stirring occasionally. Remove when the walnuts and pepitas are golden and caramelized. Sprinkle the mixture with salt and let cool on a plate.

In a large bowl, combine the baby kale or arugula, persimmons, clementines, and cranberries. Sprinkle on the burrata cheese and the walnut and pepita mixture.

For the dressing, in a separate bowl, whisk together the cranberry juice, balsamic vinegar, lemon juice, olive oil, and salt and pepper. Drizzle the dressing over the salad and enjoy.

Persimmon Sweet Potato Soup

INGREDIENTS

2 teaspoons extra virgin olive oil

2 leeks, white and green parts only, roughly chopped

3 cloves of garlic, minced

1 teaspoon grated fresh ginger

1 tablespoon curry powder

½ teaspoon paprika

¼ teaspoon cinnamon

¼ teaspoon nutmeg

1 teaspoon salt

½ teaspoon pepper

2 large sweet potatoes, peeled and chopped

4 Fuyu persimmons, peeled and chopped

1½ cups coconut milk

3 cups chicken broth

2 tablespoons almond butter

DIRECTIONS

In a large pot, heat the olive oil. Add the leeks and cook for 5 minutes, until the leeks are soft. Add the garlic, ginger, curry powder, paprika, cinnamon, nutmeg, salt, and pepper to the mixture. Cook for another minute, stirring to combine. Add the sweet potatoes, persimmons, coconut milk, chicken broth, and almond butter, then bring to a simmer and cook for 30 to 45 minutes, until the sweet potatoes are tender. Allow the soup to cool slightly, then puree until smooth.

Turmeric Persimmon Porridge

INGREDIENTS

1 cup coconut milk

2 medium persimmons

1 inch fresh ginger root, minced

½ teaspoon ground cinnamon

1 teaspoon ground turmeric

pinch of salt

1 cup rolled oats

4 tablespoons ground flax seed

Honey

DIRECTIONS

In a blender, blend the coconut milk, persimmons, ginger root, cinnamon, turmeric, and salt. Pour the mixture into a small saucepan over medium heat. Add the rolled oats and flax seed, and continually stir so the rolled oats and flax seed absorb the liquid. Cook for 10 to 20 minutes until the porridge is thick and cooked to your preferred consistency. Top with a dusting of cinnamon and a drizzle of honey to serve.

Garlic Chicken with Persimmon Salsa

INGREDIENTS

SALSA

3 Fuyu persimmons

½ teaspoon ground ginger

½ teaspoon ground cardamom

¼ teaspoon cinnamon

CHICKEN

1 teaspoon paprika

½ teaspoon smoked paprika

½ teaspoon onion powder

dash of black pepper

1 teaspoon minced garlic

2 skinless trimmed chicken breasts

DIRECTIONS

For the salsa, slice each persimmon in half. Grill the persimmon halves for about 10 minutes until soft. Add the persimmons, ginger, cardamom, and cinnamon to a food processor and pulse until you get a salsa texture.

For the chicken, in a small bowl, combine the paprika, smoked paprika, onion powder, pepper, and garlic. Rub the mixture on the chicken breasts until fully coated. Grill the chicken for about 10 minutes on each side until fully cooked, then remove and let sit for 5 minutes. Top each chicken breast with the salsa.

Spicy Persimmon Salsa

INGREDIENTS

2 cups peeled and diced Fuyu
   persimmon

½ cup chopped onion

1 jalapeño, seeded and cut into
   chunks

⅓ cup cilantro

1 tablespoon fresh lime juice

½ teaspoon salt

¼ teaspoon cayenne pepper

DIRECTIONS

Place all ingredients in a food processor and pulse until it reaches your desired consistency. It can be chunky like a traditional tomato salsa or thin and smooth—whichever you prefer. Store in the refrigerator for up to a week.

Fabulous Fuyu Persimmon Salsa

INGREDIENTS

2 small chili peppers

2 tablespoons minced ginger

¼ cup minced green onion

¼ cup chopped cilantro

2 to 3 chopped Fuyu
  persimmons

2 tablespoons lemon juice

3 tablespoons brown sugar

DIRECTIONS

Combine all ingredients in a bowl and serve on grilled chicken or fish, or simply fill a tortilla with this spicy concoction.

Persimmon Chia Pudding

CHIA PUDDING

2 cups vanilla almond milk

½ cup chia seeds

1½ teaspoons vanilla

2½ tablespoons maple syrup

½ teaspoon ground cinnamon

PERSIMMON CREAM

3 very ripe persimmons

¼ teaspoon ground cinnamon

DIRECTIONS

For the chia pudding, mix the almond milk, chia seeds, vanilla, maple syrup, and cinnamon. Pour into an airtight container and refrigerate for 8 hours.

For the persimmon cream, once the chia pudding is ready, cut the stems off the persimmons and put them into a food processor along with the cinnamon.

In four small glasses or two large glasses, create layers of the chia pudding and persimmon cream.

Persimmon Caprese Salad

INGREDIENTS

4 ripe Fuyu persimmons, cut into wedges

6 ounces fresh mozzarella, cut into small pieces

1½ cup croutons

Pomegranate seeds, to taste

10 to 14 fresh basil leaves

1 tablespoon balsamic vinegar

Salt and pepper to taste

DIRECTIONS

Toss the persimmons, mozzarella, croutons, pomegranate seeds, and basil leaves until evenly distributed. Drizzle with balsamic vinegar and season with salt and pepper.

Awesome Avocado and Persimmon Salad

INGREDIENTS

3 tablespoons olive oil

1 tablespoon wine vinegar

1 tablespoon white balsamic vinegar

1 teaspoon Dijon mustard

Salt and pepper to taste

8 cups baby arugula

1 firm Fuyu persimmon, chopped

1 avocado, cut into wedges

½ cup pomegranate seeds

DIRECTIONS

Whisk together the olive oil, vinegars, and mustard until combined. Season with the salt and pepper to taste. Toss the arugula with the dressing until well coated. Divide into serving bowls. Arrange the persimmon, avocado, and pomegranate seeds evenly over the salads.

Open Cheesy Persimmon Sandwich

Who doesn't love a grilled cheese sandwich? Well, here's an open-faced version with a persimmon-y twist. P.S. Skip the onions if it's date night.

INGREDIENTS

2 tablespoons olive oil

5 cups sliced onion

1 teaspoon sugar

1 teaspoon fresh thyme leaves

1 teaspoon pink Himalayan salt

1 teaspoon crushed black pepper

4 slices 9-grain oat bread

½ cup roasted persimmon slices

4 slices provolone cheese

DIRECTIONS

In a large skillet, heat the olive oil. Add the onion, sugar, thyme, salt, and pepper. Cover and simmer for 20 minutes. Toast the bread and top with the onions, roasted persimmons, and cheese. Place the bread in the oven on broil until the cheese is melted and serve. Serves four.

Persimmon Arugula Penne

INGREDIENTS

2½ cups peeled and cubed firm
Fuyu persimmon

1 tablespoon olive oil

½ teaspoon dried thyme

Salt and pepper to taste

8 ounces penne pasta

2 tablespoons unsalted butter

1 onion, sliced

3 cups arugula

3 tablespoons Parmesan

1 cup shredded sharp cheddar,
divided

¼ cup water

DIRECTIONS

Preheat the oven to 350 degrees. In a baking dish, toss the persimmon cubes with the olive oil. Season with thyme, salt, and pepper. Toss to combine. Bake for 30 minutes until the persimmon has softened and can be easily pierced with a fork. Set aside and let cool.

Bring a large pot of unsalted water to a boil. Cook the penne al dente according to the instructions on the package. Drain and set aside.

In a large nonstick skillet, melt the butter over medium heat. Once the butter is melted, add the sliced onion. Cook until the onion is almost translucent. Add the arugula in two portions. Cook until the arugula begins to wilt. Remove from heat and add the Parmesan and ¾ cup of the cheddar cheese. Add the roasted persimmon and cooked pasta. Toss to combine. Add ¼ cup of water, one tablespoon at a time, to moisten the pasta, until the pasta is well coated with cheese sauce. Season with salt and pepper.

Bacon-Baked Persimmon Brie

INGREDIENTS

2 strips applewood smoked bacon

¾ cup finely chopped yellow onion

2 teaspoons finely chopped fresh thyme

¾ cup diced Fuyu persimmon

¼ teaspoon cinnamon

Salt and pepper

1 (approximately ¾-pound) firm brie wedge

2 tablespoons honey

DIRECTIONS

Preheat the oven to 350 degrees and adjust a rack to the center. Line a sheet pan with parchment paper.

Place the bacon strips in a medium sauté pan and place it over medium heat. Cook the bacon on both sides until it's golden and crispy. Set aside on paper towels to drain.

Add the onion to the bacon grease in the pan. Sauté, stirring frequently, for about 10 minutes until the onions are soft and golden. Add the thyme and cook for about 30 seconds before turning the heat to low-medium. Mix in the persimmon. Crumble or chop the bacon and add it to the pan. Mix in the ¼ teaspoon of cinnamon and salt and pepper to taste, then let it cool to room temperature.

Slice the brie in half horizontally from the tip to the rind, being sure not to cut all the way through, and place it on the parchment-lined baking sheet. Gently lift the top half of the brie and add about half of the persimmon mixture in an even layer. Then spread the rest across the top. Drizzle with honey.

Place in the oven for 5 to 7 minutes, just until the cheese begins to melt. Serve with crackers or baguette slices.

Persimmon Butternut Squash Soup

INGREDIENTS

2 cups chopped butternut squash

3 medium Fuyu persimmons

8 ounces vegetable broth

1 tablespoon olive oil

1 cup coconut milk

1 tablespoon roasted almond butter

1 tablespoon maple syrup

¼ teaspoon ground cloves

½ teaspoon salt

½ teaspoon paprika

Dash of pepper

DIRECTIONS

Steam the squash until tender (60 to 90 seconds in the microwave). Then peel and chop the persimmons. Combine the persimmons, squash, and broth in a blender until smooth.

Transfer the mixture into a medium pot and add the oil, coconut milk, almond butter, and maple syrup. Place on medium-low heat and stir until combined and smooth. Then add the cloves, salt, paprika, and pepper and stir. Simmer for 30 minutes. Once the soup has thickened, stir repeatedly. Serve with an additional dash of pepper.

Persimmon Prosciutto Bites

INGREDIENTS

2 Fuyu persimmons

6 slices prosciutto

12 thin 1-inch squares cheese
  (I recommend cheddar!)

12 leaves arugula or basil

DIRECTIONS

Cut the stem ends off the persimmons and slice the persimmons. Cut the prosciutto slices in half lengthwise. Stack a slice of persimmon, a slice of cheese, and an arugula or basil leaf. Wrap the bundle with a strip of prosciutto. Repeat to make 12 bundles. Keep refrigerated until ready to serve.

Persimmon-Apple Pork Tenderloin

INGREDIENTS

3 pounds pork tenderloin

3 Fuyu persimmons, cut into large chunks

1 large apple, cut into large chunks

Salt to taste

DIRECTIONS

Put the pork in a slow cooker and cover with the persimmons, apple, and salt. Set on low and cook for 4 to 6 hours. Serve and enjoy.

Persimmon Butter

INGREDIENTS

2 pounds ripe Fuyu
  persimmons

¼ cup apple juice

1 cinnamon stick

1 teaspoon vanilla

1 teaspoon lemon juice

¼ teaspoon salt

DIRECTIONS

Peel the persimmons and cut them into ¼-inch wedges.
In a medium saucepan over medium-low heat, cook the
persimmons, stirring occasionally, with the rest of the
ingredients for 30 minutes, until the persimmons are tender.
When finished cooking, pour the mixture into a blender or
food processor. Blend until smooth.

THE PEOPLE

THE WELL-TRAVELED
PERSIMMON PUDDING

As I shared in chapter 3 of this book, when we moved to Texas for a ten-year stint for my writing career, I was desperate to find persimmon pulp—to no avail. So, once a year, my late mother-in-law, Martha Davis, would pack some of Lawrence County's best persimmon pulp into a cold shipping box and send frozen pulp for at least five persimmon puddings all the way from Bedford, Indiana, to Fort Worth, Texas. I used that pulp very selectively, savoring each pudding, knowing I wouldn't be able to get more pulp until the following year.

Apparently, I was not the only transplanted Hoosier who longed for persimmon pudding. I've heard story after story of frozen persimmon pulp and fully baked persimmon puddings making their way across the United States. My friend and transplanted Hoosier Stephanie Haverly-Koontz flew home to Indiana a few years ago to close out her storage unit and drive her belongings back to LA. She rented a big yellow Penske truck and asked her niece Heidi to join her on the cross-country adventure. They went to the Wizard of Oz museum in

Kansas, cruised the Las Vegas Strip, hiked in Arches National Park in Utah—they did it all! But most importantly, they safely transported fourteen pints of frozen persimmon pulp in a big old cooler.

"I was so excited to bring back as much pulp as I could, since we can't get persimmons out here [in LA]," Stephanie said. "I wouldn't even allow snacks in the cooler, for fear it would take up room that could be more wisely used for persimmons. We still laugh about the fun we had and how carefully we watched over the persimmons for over twenty-five hundred miles."

Now that's dedication.

Speaking of Los Angeles and its lack of American persimmons, my buddy Tammy Hammond Spradlin, one of the most talented bakers I know, makes a persimmon pudding every year and carries it through airport security so her son in LA can experience a little taste of home.

One of my high school friends, Chris Fletcher Arsenault, who has lived in Florida for a number of years, always buys persimmon pulp from Saundra, the mama of another high school friend, Gale May, whenever she is visiting Indiana. Then she carts it back to the Sunshine State—1,113 miles to Naples. She also usually makes a pit stop in Plant City, Florida, to deliver some pulp to her sister so she can also bake persimmon puddings in the fall.

"Growing up in southern Indiana, then transplanting to Florida for retirement, it's pretty hard to find those sweet persimmons here," Chris explained. "You have to get 'em when you get the opportunity." She's so right.

A DRIVE WITH A PERSIMMON-Y VIEW

For years, Ken Row commuted to the Naval Surface Warfare Center Crane Division in Martin County, Indiana, via the

Bedford gate near Silverville. Ken always enjoyed the stretch of road near the Indian Creek bridge because there, just on the edge of the woods, stood a small persimmon tree. "One of my rites of fall was watching that tree as its fruit ripened; then the leaves fell; and finally the tree would end up with a few stubborn fruits hanging on," Ken recalled.

In the early 2000s, he relocated to northern Indiana, where there were lots of lakes but nary a persimmon tree—at least along the roads he drove daily. Still, every drive during the fall kept him scanning the roadside woods for a persimmon tree only to be disappointed. Then, one day while driving through a neighboring county due to a detour, he spotted a large persimmon tree. From that day on, Ken took the detour on purpose just to see the persimmons. You've heard of taking time to smell the roses? Well, you might say Ken took the time to drive past the persimmons. Good for him. After all, it's the little things, right?

PICKING PERSIMMONS, MAKING MEMORIES

Hoosier Dorothy Haste remembers going to her uncle's place in Mitchell, Indiana, on Sundays after church in the autumn of the year. Persimmon trees grew on that property, and she and her husband, Bill, would go from tree to tree, tasting the persimmons. "It was kind of like a game," she shared. "There were different tastes from every tree. If we found a tree that had really great tasting persimmons, we would keep those persimmons separate so we could make a pudding from them. . . . Bill always removed the stems and the little black tips on the bottoms as he collected them. That was his job."

Once home, the couple would go to work. Using an aluminum cone-shaped strainer and a wooden mallet for mashing,

Dorothy and Bill extracted pulp from the sweetest persimmons of the day. The Hastes were married for fifty-four years before Bill passed away. They made lots of persimmon puddings and even more precious memories during those five-plus decades.

A PERSIMMON MIRACLE

Mildred Mullis of Lawrence County, Indiana, loved God, her family, and working on mission projects. If you were to drop by her home on any given day, you might find her carefully cutting and rolling sheets to be used as bandages overseas.

But Mildred didn't stop there. She had an idea of how she could raise money for missions—a project she would employ for many years: the persimmon project. You see, there was a healthy persimmon tree in her backyard, and Mildred knew the sweet pulp from those persimmons would bring a pretty penny in town. Every fall, she would wait for the persimmons to ripen and fall from the tree, and then she would collect them. After that, she would carefully clean the persimmons, run them through her colander, and sell the persimmon pulp to her fellow church members. This was almost a full-time job every autumn. During peak season, she would go out back and gather persimmons every hour. She didn't want to let them lie on the ground for too long, fearing they would be ruined or get buggy.

Then one year, Mildred fell ill. Late that summer, she was diagnosed with thyroid cancer and had to undergo surgery and multiple radiation treatments that she said left her "weak as a cat." But God knows his children, and he knew that despite her weakness, she would move forward with the persimmon project just like she had every fall. Her commitment to God and her missions was strong, no matter how weak she felt.

That year, the persimmon tree in her backyard that had always yielded many, many persimmons was totally barren, producing not even one persimmon. This was puzzling, since other trees dotting the nearby country roads were heavily laden with fruit. According to family member Denise Mullis, they never heard of another barren tree in the area that year. "God, in his infinite wisdom, knew she could not compete her task," Denise wrote. "He also knew that despite her debilitated state, she would try. . . . God is awesome. Thank you, Lord, for watching out for her."

IT'S A DOG EAT DOG WORLD

One of my best friends, fellow wordsmith Wendy Hinote Lanier, recently shared a story with me about her dad, Bill Hinote, and his faithful dog Bedford. It seems one of Mr. Hinote's neighbors had a couple of persimmon trees right along his fence row. After the season's first frost, Hinote and Bedford would go for a ride along the fence and stop to pick up persimmons. Bedford absolutely loved them! Of course, once you get a taste for persimmons, you just can't get enough.

Back on Hinote's land, there stood one lone persimmon tree, but one year, the deer and other animals had been quick to eat all of its fruit—all except one prime persimmon. Mrs. Hinote couldn't believe the animals had eaten all but one, and she was determined to claim it. So, as any loving husband would do, Hinote grabbed a stick and knocked the solitary persimmon out of the tree. The plan was to scoop it off the ground and deliver it to Mrs. Hinote, who was watching nearby. But that wasn't Bedford's plan. Before the persimmon even hit the ground, that darn dog caught it in his mouth and gobbled it up. Proud of his conquest, he strutted right past the Hinotes, never even looking at them. Mrs. Hinote shook her head, knowing she'd have to wait another year before she could bite into a juicy, sweet persimmon.

PERSIMMON WARS

My author friend and true southerner Linda Gilden learned of my upcoming book about persimmons and shared this childhood memory about a persimmon tree that stood at the edge of her family's yard, just where it joined their neighbor's yard, in Spartanburg, South Carolina.

"It was a pretty tree about the size of a large dogwood," she said. "At first that's what we thought it was, but it began blooming, which was followed by fruit." Linda and her siblings were intrigued by the fruit because no one ever ate it, and they wondered what it tasted like.

However, they were also a little put out by the persimmon tree because of its fruit, which they had to rake up every year—Dad's orders. "After it fell from the tree and began to rot, the fruit was messy," she remembered. "And if we stepped on it, we tracked it into the house."

One year when Linda and her sister and brother were raking the fallen fruit from around the tree, a few of the neighborhood children, who were the same ages as Linda and her siblings, stopped by.

"Whatcha doing?" one of the kids asked.

"Raking up these messy things," Linda said. "Dad is making us."

The seven-year-old neighbor picked up a persimmon. He looked around, then took aim. He hurled it toward the street light pole. *Splat!* His persimmon missile connected with its target. One of the other kids picked up a persimmon and followed suit. However, the target this time was not the streetlight pole. He hurled it toward Linda's brother! Rakes were laid down, and more persimmons began to fly. The persimmon wars had begun.

"Unfortunately, that was not the end of the persimmon wars," Linda said. "Every year when persimmons began to fall from the tree . . . it was on."

PERSIMMON PALS

For Jennifer Watts, persimmons aren't just a fruit, they're a friendship forger. You see, persimmons paved the way to a beautiful friendship between Jennifer and her coworker Michiko in Thornton, Colorado. "The only persimmon I was ever exposed to growing up was the Hachiya," Jennifer shared, noting that the Hachiya persimmon's skin could be quite bitter. So when Michiko, who is originally from Okinawa, Japan, told Jennifer you could eat a Fuyu persimmon like an apple—skin and all—it blew Jennifer's mind.

"I did not know about the sweet, succulent, taut, juicy texture of the Fuyu until I met my friend," she said. "We went to the local Asian market on our day off. She taught me how to pick out persimmons, not too hard and not too soft, and how to look for the beautiful orange amber color. Persimmons are now one of my favorite fruits!"

PERSIMMON INSPIRATION

Who knew that persimmons could inspire beautiful poetry? Well, they can, and they did. Amber Clampitt-Crane wrote this heartfelt poem in honor of her grandfather Hershel "Doodle" Willcutt and his best friends, Ed and Sue Hattabaugh, who were like second grandparents to Amber. When Ed passed away, Amber framed this poem and gave it to Sue.

Amber remembered, "We shared this nice grove of persimmon trees in Medora [Indiana] that produced the largest and sweetest fruit ever. We kept it to 'family only' for picking. The rule was, if you started picking up persimmons, you had to pick them all. I still pick persimmons there every fall. "All four of them [Doodle and Hazel Willcutt and Sue and Ed Hattabaugh] have passed on, but the tradition stays in our family. . . . I still say there are angels in my persimmon tree."

ANGELS IN MY PERSIMMON TREE
by Amber Clampitt-Crane

Down by Ed and Sue's Persimmon tree grove,
I have some special memories I have come to know.
Grandpa "Doodle" would sit on Ed's bench to tell stories of the old days
while eating his persimmons from a cottage cheese container
after a long day of baling hay.
He would split open a seed to check the winter weather forecast.
Will it be a fork, a knife, or spoon?
We watch intently to find out really soon.
Sue and I wander around under the branches
Collecting the beautiful fruits those trees would bear.
Oh, I could not wait to taste the baked goods I would make
from the pulp they were so kind to share.
We would fill a cardboard box or maybe even two,
Until they were almost too full to scoot.
Sue or Ed would also throw in some turnips to boot.
Now, I knew it was a special thing for them
to share their special treats each fall.
Especially when Ed would say,
"Now, make sure you get them all."
Our dear Ed will be missed daily in our lives
Just as my Grandpa "Doodle" is by so many.
I'll try not to be sad, for somehow I know
they'll still be around,
sending little reminders of those days
when the persimmons came falling down.
Those two "grandpa angels" are sure to be perched somewhere,
watching from the branches in those trees,
making sure they drop down the sweetest of persimmons
just for Sue and me.

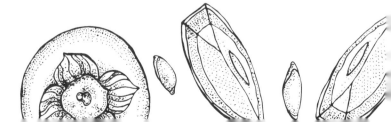

Hazel and Hershel "Doodle" Willcutt, the late persimmon connoisseurs.
Photo courtesy of Amber Clampitt-Crane.

THE PERSIMMON PUCKER

Mary Jane Sowders of Lawrence County still remembers the day she encountered a green persimmon like it was yesterday . . . and it was seventy-six years ago! She was only four at the time, and her older brother and his friend thought it would be funny to share a green persimmon with her. The two boys kept encouraging Mary Jane to take a bite, so the unsuspecting little girl sunk her teeth into the not-yet-ripened fruit. "I can still taste that persimmon like I just put it into my mouth," she said. "It was horrible." Most people growing up in Indiana know that there's nothing sourer than a green persimmon. Mary Jane learned that truth the hard way.

A SORE END

Bill and Joyce Sipes are not only husband and wife, they are also persimmon lovers. Every autumn, they go to Bill's mother's house in Indiana to gather the sweetest persimmons. This past fall, the twosome went to Bill's mom's house once again, and they were pleasantly surprised by the many persimmons awaiting them. One by one the couple picked the fruit, almost filling the basket Bill was toting. Just when they thought they'd snagged every last persimmon on the ground, Joyce thought she spotted another one lying between two trees growing in a small incline in the yard. Not wanting to leave even one persimmon behind, Joyce reached for it. But in the process, she lost her balance and tumbled down the hill, nearly breaking her tailbone.

After she regained her bearings, she looked up to see Bill standing nearby. In fact, she had tumbled right past him. She couldn't believe it. "Bill! Why didn't you try to catch me?" she insisted.

Her loving husband smiled and said, "Because I didn't want to drop my basket of persimmons." Yep. Hoosiers take their persimmons seriously.

epilogue

𝒜 t's been proven that the sense of smell is closely linked with memory, probably more so than any of our other senses. Maybe that's why I love the smell of baking persimmon pudding so much. As I inhale that marvelous aroma, I'm reminded of so many wonderful family gatherings, and I'm excited about all the get-togethers to come.

Food has always had a way of connecting us with friends and family. In our house, the kitchen is where many meaningful discussions take place. (Yeah, we've pretty much solved all the world's problems sitting at the table or leaning against the kitchen bar.) And it's the place where we goof around, dance in our socks, and occasionally play a game of euchre at the table my parents bought my husband and I when we were first married. The kitchen, you might say, is a magical place in our home. I don't necessarily love to cook—I like to *have cooked* so we can all enjoy the fruits of my labor. Maybe you can relate.

As my husband and I settle into the current empty-nest phase of our lives, the years seem to race by. Seasons change. Years pass. Loved ones pass on. Kids grow up and move out, get married, have children of their own, and hopefully visit often. Old friends and new friends gather for parties year after year. The little things become the big things, and I find myself appreciating the simple pleasures I might have taken for granted in my twenties and thirties.

Persimmon pudding, my friends, is one of those simple pleasures. It's a comfort food but not for the reasons you might think. Sure, any dessert is technically a comfort food, I suppose. But persimmon pudding is a comfort food because fall after fall, year after year, family gathering after family gathering, it remains a constant. It's like an old friend you're always glad to see. It never disappoints.

It's my hope that you'll come to love some of the recipes in this book as much as I do. I hope you'll find a signature dish or two that will entice your family and friends into your kitchen for important talk and utter silliness. And I hope the persimmon—whether you're making persimmon cookies for a bake sale or persimmon fudge for your daughter's after-prom gathering—becomes that go-to comfort food for you and yours.

Last, don't wait for a special occasion to celebrate—live, bake, eat, and be happy! It's like that country song by Old Dominion says: "Life is short. Make it sweet."

NOTES

1. THE HISTORY, THE VARIETIES, THE LORE

1. Chapter 11. Lenny D. Farlee, "The Fruit of the Gods from an Indiana Tree?" Purdue Extension Forestry and Natural Resources, last modified September 5, 2018, https://www.purdue.edu/fnr /extension/blog/2018/09/05/the-fruit-of-the-gods-from-an-indiana -tree/.

2. Raymond A. Sokolov, *Fading Feast: A Compendium of Disappearing American Regional Foods* (Jaffrey, NH: David R. Godine, 1998), 26.

3. "Eating Seasonally: Persimmons," CUESA, accessed July 22, 2019, https://cuesa.org/food/persimmons.

4. "American Persimmon (*Diospyros virginiana*)," The Fruit Nut, last modified March 3, 2014, https://thefruitnut.com/american -persimmon/.

5. Susan Patterson, "Persimmon Tree Care: Learn How to Grow Persimmon Trees," Gardening Know How, last modified April 26, 2018, https://www.gardeningknowhow.com/edible/fruits/persimmon /growing-persimmon-trees.htm.

6. "The Difference between Hachiya and Fuyu Persimmons," GreenBlender, accessed July 24, 2019, https://greenblender.com /smoothies/7202/difference-between-hachiya-and-fuyu -persimmons.

7. Francis Skalicky, "Facts of Persimmons as Interesting as Folklore," *Springfield News-Leader* (Missouri), October 5, 2018, https:// www.news-leader.com/story/sports/outdoors/2018/10/05/facts -persimmons-interesting-folklore/1486574002/.

8. L. Joyce Mundy, "Persimmons Fed Early Settlers," *Times-Mail* (Bedford, IN), September 25, 2018, A3–A5.

9. "Raccoon and the Persimmon," Crawdad Creek Wildlife Rehab, accessed July 24, 2019, http://www.oocities.org/crawdad creekrehab/RaccoonPersimmon.html.

10. "Korean Folklore: The Tiger and the Persimmon," The Kraze, January 13, 2019, http://www.thekrazemagazine.com/latest-updates /2019/1/13/korean-folklore-the-tiger-and-the-persimmon.

11. "Persimmon Coffee," *Montgomery Advertiser* (Alabama), November 18, 1863.

12. George Ray McEachern and B. G. Hancock, "Texas Persimmons," Aggie Horticulture, January 27, 1997, https://aggie -horticulture.tamu.edu/extension/fruit/Persimmons/persimmons .html.

2. A TALE OF TWO FESTIVALS

1. "The Best Food Festival in Every US State," *National Geographic*, July 20, 2016, https://www.nationalgeographic.com/travel/travel -interests/food-and-drink/top-food-festival-every-US-state/?fbclid =IwAR3hErsTXtyZBetYhhFM5r5deVR5-aee-5BdlE43YKQ9Ybx 7ru0DKe4GDaM.

*M*ichelle Medlock Adams is an award-winning journalist and best-selling author. She has earned top honors from the Associated Press, the Society of Professional Journalists, the Hoosier State Press Association, the Selah Awards, the Golden Scrolls, the Maxwell Awards, and the Illumination Awards. But she is yet to win a medal for "Best Persimmon Pudding," which is on her bucket list, so she plans to enter for the first time this year.

Since graduating with a journalism degree from Indiana University, Michelle has written and published over ninety books, with close to four million books sold. She has also written more than 1,500 articles for newspapers, magazines, and websites; acted as a stringer for the Associated Press; written for a worldwide ministry; helped pen a *New York Times* best seller; hosted *Joy in Our Town* for the Trinity Broadcasting Network; blogged twice weekly for *Guideposts* from 2013 to 2015; written a weekly column for a Midwest newspaper; and served as an adjunct professor at Taylor University three different years. Today, she is president of Platinum Literary Services, a premier full-service literary firm; chairman of the board of advisors for Serious Writer

Inc.; an online instructor for the Serious Writer Academy; and a much sought-after speaker at writers' conferences and women's retreats all over the United States. When not working on her own assignments, Michelle ghostwrites articles, blog posts, and books for celebrities, politicians, and some of today's most effective and popular ministers. She is currently celebrating the recent release of her books *Dinosaur Devotions*, *What Is America?*, *They Call Me Mom*, and *Platinum Faith*.

Michelle is married to her high school sweetheart, Jeff. They have two daughters, Abby and Allyson, two sons-in-law, one grandson, and two granddaughters. (And they all love persimmon pudding!) She and Jeff share their home in southern Indiana with a miniature dachshund, a rescue shepherd/collie mix, and two cats. When not writing or teaching writing, Michelle enjoys hiking the Milwaukee Trail, bass fishing, and cheering on the Indiana University sports teams and the Chicago Cubbies. To learn more about Michelle, sign up for her newsletter, or, to read her weekly blog, go to michellemedlockadams.com.